THE GRAEME PULLEN GUIDE TO
Sea Fishing Baits

The Oxford Illustrated Press

The Oxford Illustrated Press

© Graeme Pullen, 1988

ISBN 0 946609 74 8

Published by:
The Oxford Illustrated Press Limited, Haynes Publishing Group, Sparkford, Nr Yeovil, Somerset BA22 7JJ, England.

Haynes Publications Inc., 861 Lawrence Drive, Newbury Park, California 91320, USA.

Printed in England by:
J.H. Haynes & Co Limited, Sparkford, Nr. Yeovil, Somerset.

British Library Cataloguing in Publication Data
Pullen, Graeme
   Sea fishing baits.
   1. Sea angling. Baits
   1. Title
   799.1'6

ISBN 0-946609-74-8

Library of Congress Catalog Card Number
88-80362

All rights reserved. No part of this book may be reproduced or transmitted in any form or by any means, electronic or mechanical, including photocopying, recording or by any information storage retrieval system, without the permission of the publisher.

Contents

Introduction	5
Cockles	7
Mussels	9
Whelks	12
Limpets	14
Razorfish	26
Whitebait	29
Prawns	30
Shrimps	33
Small Fish	34
Sprats	36
Sandeels	38
Herring	52
Smelt	55
Pilchard	56
Pouting and Poor Cod	57
Mackerel	60
Lugworm	74
Ragworm	80
Squid	88
Octopus	100
Cuttlefish	101
Crabs	102
Artificials	109
Bait Additives	120
Appendix	124

Acknowledgements

I must acknowledge all those charter skippers who have given me pleasant days afloat plus Tony Kirrage and Norman Message of 'Tony's Tackle Team' in Eastbourne, for their assistance and tips on shore fishing. Also my old Adler Universal 200 typewriter for getting me through another book without having to resort to the purchase of a word processor!

Dedication

To the future generation of anglers.
Clear skies. Clean seas. Tight lines.

Introduction

For many anglers, be they saltwater or freshwater anglers, acquisition and storage of bait is not only a necessity, but a pleasurable activity in itself. Certainly if you want to enjoy any sort of success in your fishing you must use the right bait and match it correctly to the species you want to hook. Bait gathering can be simple if you are a freshwater angler because most of the baits (with the exception of the bloodworm) are either land based, or come out of a carton or tin and can be bought from your local tackle shop or supermarket.

The sea angler however, has the problem that all of his baits are true 'naturals' and must either be collected from the sea itself or gathered at low water when parts of the sea bed are uncovered. To this extent, exactly when the saltwater man can gather his sea-bed baits is entirely governed by the actions and times of the tide. With some baits, such as black lugworm or razorfish, this timing can be critical in as much as they can only be gathered from that section of the sea bed which is exposed only on low water springs—and even then gathering time is limited to a couple of hours before the tide comes in again.

I for one regard the energetic use of a deep black lug spade as something worth avoiding. Professional bait diggers operate all around the country to supply tackle shops with bait and although it is not cheap, next time you complain about the cost, think about the effort that has been involved—such as digging bait at the unsociable hour of five o'clock in the morning!

If you can't find the time to catch and store fresh sea baits you can of course always walk into your local fish shop or tackle shop and purchase some there. At least both these outlets offer you instant bait, but remember that you simply cannot beat fresh, well-looked-after bait for catching either a quantity of fish or a single large specimen.

There are literally hundreds of permutations between baits of different colourings, flavourings and shapes. This book is not intended to be a dictionary of every single bait known to man, it is more a guide to those baits that are relatively easy to obtain, and which in my own experience can result in a high success rate of both

Sea Fishing Baits

quantity and quality.

So far, by travelling abroad to extend my own fishing capabilities and knowledge, I have taken some 200 different species, and many on the baits included in this book. Hopefully, by using this book, you too may boost your catch rate, and in doing so gain even more pleasure from this enjoyable sport of ours.

Cockles

I do not intend boring you with a detailed breakdown of every single burrowing bivalve, its latin name or even how often it reproduces. Scientific books exist elsewhere that list that type of information, and you have my word that being able to recite all their names will not boost your catch rate.

Cockles are a bivalve that live primarily in sand, and whilst they're not the best bait you can use, they are useful for small fish like pouting, dabs, rockling, small codling, whiting and plaice. After a good storm they are easy to find, presumably because they have been dislodged from the sand by the sea and pounded about in the surf zone. They are recognisable by their orange colour and the red piece of flesh known as the 'foot'. Difficult to keep alive, except maybe with a bucket of seawater and an aerator, they are best frozen down immediately after they have been collected. They are one of the tougher shellfish to get on the hook, but keep things small—you don't want a great 4/0 hook showing with a tiny piece of cockle on the neck of the bend, better instead to use a freshwater number 2 carp hook; this is sufficient for a couple of cockles, and is more easily taken by the flatfish.

If you decide to go out and collect your own cockles you'll need a pair of waders (the thigh type or even chest waders) and to get out at low water springs to look for them. Occasionally they can be collected on low water neap tides, but the springs uncover them better. As soon as they're gathered, take them out of the shell, drop them in a bucket of water, add some salt, and when you get home, shake them out onto some newspaper and roll them around to get off any excess moisture and salt. Then put them in a plastic bag or container and put them in the freezer. Because they are small they don't take long to defrost so you can use them at the last moment, if necessary, and even bring them back from your fishing trip and re-freeze them if you take a cool box with you.

Aside from the unusual big cockle of three inches or so which can sometimes be found and then used on its own for bass, it is more likely that you will need at least a bunch of six cockles if you are bassing or winter cod fishing. Use elastic thread to bind them on the hook. As a guideline for those who like eating cockles, a rich bed may

Sea Fishing Baits

contain over a million to the acre. The cockle feeds by digging its foot into the sand and using it as a lever to bury itself. Then, using its two siphons it draws sea water and food in through one end and out through the other. The shell is ridged and care should be taken when scooping the meat out to avoid leaving yourself with a ragged bait; use a blunt, round-tipped kitchen knife to get them out.

One thing I have found with cockles is that you rarely have to fish them a long way out. While distance casting is all the vogue, many anglers forget the cockle lives close to the low water mark. If there is not a great expanse of tide from low to high water, a cast behind the surf line is ideal. Remember that the fish are only able to feed on the cockles when they have been dislodged during a gale. The shells that are dumped as 'empties' on the beach have had to be pounded through the littoral, or food zone. The other factor to remember is that you will presumably be using them to catch flatfish anyway, and to retain any sort of sport, you would surely only need a rod blank that throws two or three ounces? Why heave out six ounces, when you can fish close in with a set of light tackle?

As a standby winter bait, $1/4$lb of frozen cockles are always worth having. Most tackle shops won't stock them, and although they are available from supermarkets, why not take advantage of low water and check out the beach and collect cockles at the same time?

Mussels

As the old song goes, 'Cockles and Mussels, Alive, Alive- O!' Like cockles, mussels have long been enjoyed by humans as a tasty snack especially when eaten with salt and vinegar. Mussels are usually not too difficult to find, and grow in beds on the sea floor. They like rough ground rather than an open surf beach, and so you should look for them under piers or rocks, by harbour walls and jetties. They are found near the low water mark, and attach themselves in clumps that make removal difficult. They can be mixed in with barnacles, so don't go tearing at them with your bare hands or you will get cut fingers. They also like old sewage outflow pipes, and when collecting them from these you should take special care, particularly if you have any open cuts on your hands.

Even though the mussel has a large and hard shell, the meat inside is small. The edible variety has a dark blue shell and is usually in the region of three inches long. The hinge of the shell is very strong, and must be opened with a blunt knife in a similar way to cockles. Once inside, you will find the meat much softer than a cockle's, and because of this you must use elasticated thread to bind it to the hook. No matter how well you do it though, pieces of mussel will still fly off the hook during the cast, so put on more than you would normally use to allow for some loss.

Some anglers say the only way to get them to stay on the hook is by putting the hook through the foot, but even that is soft. One of the better ways is to rig up with a small pair of double hooks, instead of the large single. Finer wire will stop it tearing so much.

A good chunk of mussel meat, whipped to the hook with thread, will bring you cod in the winter, bass in the summer, and even huge pouting which have a prodigous appetite when it comes to consuming that soft mussel meat.

Mussels do not freeze down well, and I advise using them the same day, or night that you collect them. Extract them from the shell and drop into a small bait tin lined with newspaper to soak up excess moisture, then remove from the paper and leave them in an ordinary plastic bait box. They keep better by leaving them in the shell after you have collected them, just covering with wet seaweed. This way they can be kept for as long as a week, provided you keep them in a

Sea Fishing Baits

This cod had been feeding heavily on crabs that lived over the mussel beds. A big mussel bait will often pick up good cod, but being such a soft bait it should be tied to the hookshank using elasticated cotton.

Mussels

It's lunkers like this big shore cod, taken by the author from Waxham beach in Norfolk, that respond best to a big bait like a bunch of mussels. Although primarily a worm area, the Norfolk and Suffolk surf beaches respond well to the angler specialising in mussel baits.

cool place, and change the seaweed regularly. The shell lids fit together very tightly and this seems to enable them to retain their own body moisture for longer than other shellfish. You'll certainly know when they have died and decomposed, as will every other angler downwind of you.

One particular use I have found for soft mussels, is that they are excellent when used crushed up for harbour mullet. The particles of meat sink slowly, attracting a wide variety of small harbour-dwelling fish like pouting, rockling and even scad. Mashed mussels are best mixed with bran and a little pilchard oil when used for groundbait. The best part for a mullet hookbait is the foot, but make sure you use small hooks.

Whelks

In complete contrast to the soft flesh of the mussel and cockle, that of the whelk is tough and as a bait it is not only unlikely to fly off the hook during the cast, but is difficult to get on in the first place. The whelk is a rubbery shellfish that is easily identified by the tapering swirl of shell which is its home. The largest of the dog whelks, it is known as the dog winkle, and feeds on mussels or even barnacles. It is something of a chameleon in the shellfish world, as it has the ability to slightly change its colour depending on what it is feeding on. I said that the whelk is a tough customer and its diet certainly confirms this. Barnacles are hard at the best of times but a whelk kills them by inserting a poison, then prising the shells apart to get at the barnacle inside.

The common whelk, which can be several inches long, can occasionally be collected near mussel beds at low tide. They make ideal big bass and cod baits in the summer, resisting the nippy little claws of the summer crabs. A pest on the oyster beds is another variety called the sting winkle, which drills away at the shells to get at the occupants within. Finally there is the netted dog whelk, a lot smaller and unlikely to be of much use to the angler.

There is no easy way to get a strong-muscled whelk out of the shell. Forget the blunt kitchen knife and approach with a small hammer, cracking the shell away carefully to reveal, but not damage, the meat within. A good sized whelk can be cut into several different baits and when cut into tiny rubbery strips it will attract small fish like pouting. The one drawback in using a whole one is that you need an oversize hook to keep the point clear of the meat. For this reason it is better to cut it in half, lengthwise. You can then place the hook through one half, bind to the eye of the hook with elasticated cotton, and leave the other half hanging loosely. While I don't believe there is any fish swimming that feeds directly on a whelk, I feel fish move in on whatever is in front of them. The floor of the seabed is a far from easy place to scrape a living (made more difficult by the damage caused to the seabed by trawler chains), so competition for food is very high. Therefore if a piece of whelk is there, even though a fish may never have seen one before outside of its shell, it will smell good and so the fish will be attracted to it.

Whelks

Whelks may not be collectable from the shoreline in vast quantities, so either buy them from your fishmongers or check with some of the commercial clam, scallop and oyster boats to see if they have dredged any up. They can be frozen after salting or simply kept in wet seaweed for a few days. In fact even when they are half decomposed they still seem pretty tough.

The use of the whelk must surely be as that of a standby, but be advised that they are a good bait though, and it never hurts to keep a few to try when you come across them.

Limpets

Here is a true shoreline bait that can be gathered by anybody. There are two types of limpet: the circular ones that can be found clinging to rocks and harbour walls near the low-water mark, and the round-backed slipper limpets that cling to each other's backs. There is a knack to gathering them though and the age-old saying 'cling like a limpet' could never be truer. To collect what I shall term the rock limpet is a job for the quick of hand. These limpets cling to the rocks quite gently until you come along looking for bait. Then at the first touch of its shell you will see it suck down and grip the face of the rock with incredible power, and try as you might, should you miss it at the first attempt you'll probably end up smashing the shell in your rage. The knack lies in one firm hard whack sideways with a piece of wood or rock to knock it off before it gets a chance to grip down on the moist rock. Once removed the limpet is a tough bait that is especially good for wrasse.

I won't say they are a super bait, but their rubbery texture means that at least they stay on the hook well. As for keeping them, simply take them out of the shell using a blunt ended kitchen knife, roll in salt and freeze down. They dehydrate like all frozen items, but the salt makes them as tough as old boot leather. An alternative to freezing is to cover them in wet seaweed while they're still in their shells – then they will keep for several days.

I personally go for the larger ones, and cut them into two or three strips to facilitate ease of hooking, and for better bait presentation. Limpets are univalves as opposed to bivalves, and therefore possess a larger sucker foot which makes them good for hookbaits.

The slipper limpet is found in groups and often as many as nine or ten can be picked up clinging to each other. Alternatively you may find them clinging to stones or kelp which have been torn loose by wild gales and lashing seas, forcing them to break free from the seabed, and carrying the slipper limpets with them. Once into the littoral zone the limpets are pounded by the surf which dislodges them and they then become an important part of the food chain. I have found many shingle beaches most productive for collecting baits after a gale during spring tides. This I feel is due to the fact that the surf line of pounding waves is farther out during spring tides, and

The author punches out a clump of slipper limpets from Hayling beach front. Generally such flat conditions produce little, so why not take the opportunity to spice them up with an extra big helping of bait, or even a cocktail of several baits?

breaks free weed and rocks not normally disturbed by a gale on neap tides.

The fishing after such a blow can be excellent, especially for winter flounders that take full advantage of this new found food supply. I have often fished one rod baited with worm and another with slipper

Sea Fishing Baits

These are slipper limpets, and on the right side of the photo you can see how they suction on the back of each other's shell. Lever them apart using a blunt knife and gently scoop out the meat for hookbait.

limpets after such a storm, and seen the limpets consistently the most productive. Remember that most of the dislodged limpets will be rolling about in the littoral zone so a simple 30 to 60 yards cast is sufficient distance. Don't go for anything more or you will be casting over the heads of the fish. It's always difficult to preach close-in fishing to an angler proudly displaying his 'I can cast 500 yards' badge, but if you fish where the feeding zone is and not where current casting fashion dictates, you should always outfish them!

Slipper limpets can be collected along the high-tide line or along the water line, amongst clumps of kelp and weed-covered stones. Extract them from their shells, dry them, add salt as a toughener and freeze them down for future use.

Using a bait that comes from the area you are fishing and is directly available to the fish after a good storm cannot be bettered. In this case the author took this huge haul of flounders and dabs from Hayling Island on slipper limpet and ragworm cocktails. The largest flounder weighed 2lb 4oz.

Sprats are obtainable from either the fishmonger's slab, or from a local trawl boat if you have a contact. They have little smell but can be spiced up by adding pilchard oil, or one of the cyalume chemical lightsticks. These fish are anchovies caught by nets in America, and are the equivalent to our own sprats.

Whitebait can be loosely termed as any small fish fry though most are the young of herring and sprats. They form an important part of all predator diets.

A whelk on its own (left) is one of the most durable hookbaits, and once the empty shell is discarded, a hermit crab will take up residence (right). Hermit crabs are excellent for cod and whiting.

This shows the difference in size between the Greater Sandeel or Launce (top), and the two ordinary Lesser Sandeels (below). The smaller eels are generally more productive.

Sandeels and Launce have enormous telescopic mouths, and will attack small fish and shrimps in their quest for food. The jaw membrane is almost like clear, thin plastic.

The greater Sandeel is also known as the Launce, and is at least twice as big as the Lesser Sandeel. They are best used when thin fillets are taken off each flank.

Above: A mackerel fished whole will be the best bait for big blue shark, like this 70-lb fish taken by Nigel Newport off the Irish shark point of Courtmacsherry.

Left: The mackerel is our finest and most popular boat fishing bait. To get the maximum number of baits from one fish, follow this procedure . . .

Top right: Holding the head of the mackerel, take a sharp filleting knife and make your first cut right behind the pectoral fin.

Middle: Run the knife in a gentle slicing motion down the entire flank, not cutting the backbone, but running the blade edge along it in a stroking motion.

Bottom: Bring the knife out as near the tail as possible and you have an entire fillet with meat and blood on, used primarily for big fish.

Above: If mackerel are at a premium or you want smaller species, then simply split each of those large flank fillets down the centre. You can use the lateral line as a guide, and remember to cut all baits into the flesh side, with the scaled side lying on the cutting board.

Left: Do the same with the other flank to give you two baits, and slice off that thin white strip of meat remaining on the belly. That piece is the best bait for turbot fishing with a long flowing trace.

Facing page: The 'Split-tail' mackerel is the author's favourite bait for shallow-water tope. This thirty pounder took his bait in Blacksod Bay, Ireland, and was tagged and returned alive for future research.

Above: My personal favourite big bait for predators like tope, conger, skate and even shark is what I popularised as the 'Split-tail'. Some anglers call it a flapper. It consists of slicing the backbone out, to leave a soft, limp bait, but remember to sever the backbone as near to the head as possible.

Left: By careful use with a sharp knife you can actually take nine strip baits of a good size from the one mackerel, plus of course you can use the head and guts for conger.

Limpets

For flatfish keep the hooks small, and not too long in the shank. For whiting, bass and cod you'll need three or four held on the hook with elasticated thread. Of the two types, I would say the softer slipper limpet is by far the better bait.

Facing page: A tiny strip bait of silver mackerel belly will account for every species at some time or other. This beautiful red gurnard found the author's offer irresistible!

Razorfish

Razorfish is about the best shellfish bait you can get. With this you can take bass, flounders, cod, dabs, plaice, dogfish, whiting and even pollock. It's rare to find it available from your local tackle shop, but if you frequent one that is supplied by a professional digger, it would be in your interest to see if he can get you some. Unfortunately for the angler, they are generally only collected at very low water spring tides, when the last of the sand is left exposed. This is not necessarily just after Sunday lunchtime when the sun is shining, so be prepared to get up in the middle of the night if that is the best time to catch low tide.

Razorfish are a deep boring shellfish and there are two varieties, both of which grow from 3 to 7 inches in length—large enough for an angler's hookbait. They can be seen with a tiny tip protruding above the sand at very low water, but are highly sensitive to vibration and disappear from sight in a second. They bury themselves straight down, and the only way to successfully get them out is by hard, fast digging. One old method of procuring them is to pour some table salt down the hole into which they disappear and to grab them with a pronged fork when they pop their heads up.

To find them, walk quietly over the sand, picking the cleanest area possible, and tread slowly and carefully. If you cannot actually see their holes, you will have to wait until you see a tiny spurt of water which will indicate the place where they are burying themselves in an effort to get away from you. Mark the spot mentally, then get digging quickly, straight down to at least a spit and a half of the blade. The foot that the razor uses to lever itself away from you at such speed is the bit you want, so don't try to grab it unless you have it out on the spade in one lift. If you do you will snap off the foot and be left with the softer top half of the razor.

They can also be speared on moonlit nights, or by using an Anchor pressure lamp. They seem to stick their siphons out of their burrows further at night, and a careful jab with a long-handled fork will be less strenuous than digging. It takes practice though, so be prepared to miss quite a few when you first start.

As for keeping them, simply leave them in their shell and cover with damp seaweed. If you place a layer of seaweed in between the

Razorfish

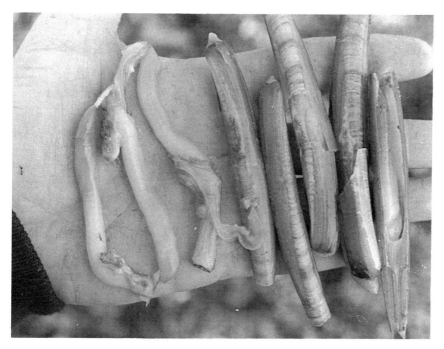

After a good storm, a bait of razorfish is hard to beat from a shore angler's point of view. The white finger of meat is taken out of the shells and mounted on a fine-wire Aberdeen hook. Excellent for bass and big flatfish.

razorfish (I have even heard of wet corrugated paper being used), you can stack them several layers high, and still keep them alive. In this manner you can keep them for up to a week if you keep them cool, but don't leave dead razors in with the live ones or you will lose the lot. Replace the seaweed or damp corrugated paper every day.

To use the razors, carefully remove them by slitting along the edge of the shell to extract the white meat and foot within. Many say the only part worth using is the muscled foot, but I feel this is because they think the softer body tissue simply flies off the hook. For this reason I only fish them on a long shank hook, usually a blued Aberdeen, which allows me to thread the whole razorfish over the point, and up round the bend, to support the whole body. You may

Sea Fishing Baits

need a tiny bait-retaining second hook if you fish two razors in this fashion, to stop them sliding down to the bend of the hook.

If you use hook or bait clips it's possible to cast them well out, but as mentioned before, most fish are likely to come across razorfish after a good storm when they have been pounded out from their burrows by the heavy wave action, and are being washed around.

I have frozen them down, but they are one of those shellfish baits that are far, far better when used fresh.

Whitebait

Whitebait is something that almost every fish must come across at one time or another, yet it is rare to see an angler using it as bait. You can buy it from your local fishmongers, you can freeze it down and you can flavour it with pilchard oil. Basically whitebait or brit as it was known years ago, is the fry stage of many of our main pelagic species like herring, pilchards and sprats. They are more popular during the summer months when the pelagics have spawned and there are plenty of whitebait shoals around for other species to eat. Next time you are out in a boat busy feathering up some mackerel, spare a thought for what your feathers are supposed to be imitating. Yes, small live fish, or whitebait. I have seen vast shoals of fry harvested by commercial bait fishermen from the warm shallow waters in Bermuda and the Florida Keys, but sadly we lack warm waters over here, so have to rely on the fish shops for our supply.

A couple of pounds of good whitebait, when mixed with bran and pilchard oil is an excellent attractant for harbour pollock, mackerel and garfish, and would doubtless have the same effect out at sea. Loose handfuls are thrown in until you are confident there are some predators about, then using float tackle, you cast in with either a single or double fry on a small hook—a size 10 freshwater will suffice.

Whitebait can't really be used as a serious casting bait, but out from a boat they can be dropped carefully down to the bottom to be taken by a wider variety of species, including wrasse. The noble bass is a prime predator of whitebait, yet I have never heard of an angler catching one on this bait from a boat, but maybe this method would work. In the States they regularly chum or groundbait up predators from boats using fry as both groundbait and hookbait. Catches made when a shoal of predators like bluefish are located, can be tremendous, so maybe there is a method of chumming with whitebait that has yet to be fully exploited over here. A good method is to rig a paternoster consisting of three single hooks, each with a whitebait on, and floatfishing it in your groundbaited area. This multiplies your chance of a take. I have heard of vast quantities of small fry being taken from the screens of power stations, so this may be both a good supply and an excellent place to try. Try whitebait at least once in the summer; certainly it can be called a little-known bait!

Prawns

Whereas crabs are the primary bottom food for most species of scavenging fish, the prawn is available to those species that swim a little higher in the water. Some areas have none, while others can host a super abundance of this high protein food source. They are one of the most popular baits in the States, and may be found readily in American tackle shops. The prawn is probably the number one bait for the shallow water 'flats' fisherman in the Florida Keys where they are used both live and dead to take many of the top gamefish. Bonefish, permit, tarpon, snook, sharks and even stingray are among the species that feed on the prawns. They are more likely to be called shrimps in the States but are as large as the British homegrown prawns. The American tackle shops keep them for customers, by putting them in a large aerated tank where they can be kept for over a week, the dead ones being taken out and frozen down for chum, or groundbait. These are caught in fine mesh nets set by a rowing boat.

British prawns must be obtained either from the fishmonger or by wading into low-water rock pools and catching them individually with a dip net. This is not as easy as it sounds and requires an expert hand. You need to dip the net on the underside of any kelp or weed that is still partially covered by seawater and lift out the net slowly, dragging it along the edge of the weed. If there are rock ledges, ease the net underneath, for many prawns live in these tiny crevices and will scurry away at the approach of the net. They generally move out with an ebb tide, and are well known for moving inshore to feed with an incoming tide. The inside of harbour walls and jetties is another good place to try, especially since you can get a smooth sweep of the net along the edge of the concrete.

Another, easier, way to collect them is while you are actually fishing. The prawns are more active during the hours of darkness, and can be taken with the aid of a drop net. The net is slightly weighted with a small rock, baited with a mackerel skeleton, and lowered to the rocks below. Remember to tie the skeleton to the net with a piece of nylon, otherwise a crab may drag it off. Leave the net down for at least fifteen minutes, resisting the temptation to keep lifting it up to see what is caught. Let it settle on the bait, then bring the net up quickly in overhand pulls. Don't stop otherwise the

Prawns

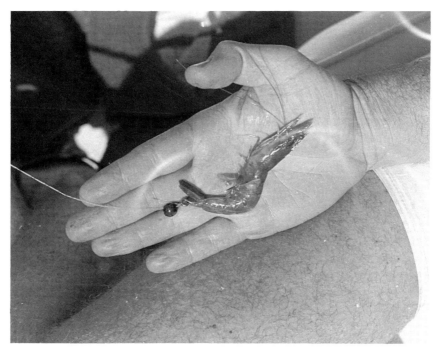

Shrimps or prawns are best used for inshore work where the fish are feeding around pilings, jetties or off deep-water rocky headlands. Mounted on a single hook, with a swan shot for weight, they can be deadly when freelined or floatfished in a swell.

prawns will escape.

Another way to catch them, although I confess to not having much luck with it, is by trapping. An old biscuit tin should have a few holes punched in it large enough for a prawn to get through. Weight it with a stone or rock, tie some string to it, add some old fish offal and drop it down. This is best left overnight, but really I think that wading and netting your own, or drop-netting from rocks or harbours is a far better way to procure them.

You can keep them alive if you intend using them the same day you catch them, by placing them in a bucket with a small battery-powered aerator. I would advise keeping them alive as long as possible, and

Sea Fishing Baits

should you have any left, freeze them in plastic bags while still alive. They are almost as successful when fished dead as they are live. Many prawn fishermen, when fishing for wrasse, believe you should leave the shell on. However I have found it far better to peel them and just use the meat on the hook. That way you can strike at the first sign of a bite and be sure of a good hookhold.

There are several species of prawn and there is even one that can change colour to suit its environment like a chameleon. Don't forget to have a look in any brackish water in estuaries as prawns come in here to feed, as well as in the open sea. Don't use too heavy a gauge wire in your hooks as this will break the meat up. Stick to fine wire and the prawns will stay on better.

For me the place for prawn fishing is a rocky headland with some tide, allowing one to trot the float round in search of pollock, mackerel and wrasse. Few baits are more effective in high summer than prawns.

Shrimps

Shrimps are a smaller cousin of the prawn, but live in a slightly different habitat. Whereas the prawn lives around kelp beds in rock pools, the shrimps comes from the 'plains' of open sandy beaches. It buries itself in the sand to feed with the tips of its feelers sticking out. Shrimps can be seen in clear sand pools but quickly disappear into the bottom, making you wonder if you really saw them at all.

To catch them, make up a wide rim net in the shape of a 'V' with a straight bar along the front, and mount it with a fine mesh net. Gently bump it along the bottom of the sand to disturb the shrimps but do it in one quick movement otherwise they will dart out again.

A far easier way is to buy the shrimps from your local fishmonger, for like prawns, they work just as well dead, as alive. The brown variety of shrimps is best, and a pint is more than enough for a day's floatfishing. Make sure you peel them first, a tricky operation but one that allows an instant strike should you get a bite.

A useful tip with this bait, is that it makes superb chum and groundbait when crushed up with some breadcrumb groundbait for mullet. Use a piece of shrimp on a size 10 freshwater hook and floatfish amongst the groundbait only when you have seen signs of mullet feeding. Although this fish is generally secretive about what it eats, a tasty shrimp seems to make it lose all caution, and you get a good bite.

Keep any shrimps cool in a cooler box if possible, as they go off very quickly in the sun, and then the meat will be too soft to stay on the hook. Shrimps are alright for groundbait, next to useless as hookbaits, not particularly good as a bait on the bottom as it doesn't stand up too well to the ravages of the crabs, but as a suspended or floatfished bait, it's another weapon in your armoury!

Small Fish

Many anglers forget at times that all sea fish are predators. They may be predatory in the sense that they feed directly on a small fry or live fish, or they may scavenge on a dead fish. No angler wants to start baiting up with decomposing fish, but there are one or two live fish that can be gathered while prawn netting, that make good baits. Blennies and rock goby live in the same habitat as the prawn—that of heavily weeded rock pools—and it is fair to assume that the larger fish in the food chain, such as pollock, bass and cod, will come across them as they forage about for prawns and crabs. For this reason it is worth trying to catch a few of these 'bonus' baits while you are already engaged in the gathering of prawns.

The blennies and butterfish are quite small, anything from three to five inches long. They can often be seen if you peer quietly into a rock pool, where they drift about, often stopping to rest by balancing on their fins. The butterfly blenny is larger, growing to 7 inches, but it is the 3-inch fish you want to keep for bait. My first discovery that these small fish were often successful as bait, came while I was wrasse fishing in the Isles of Scilly. While there I spent a good two hours at low water near Hugh Town on St Mary's collecting hardback crabs for bait but on this occasion I decided to keep three or four of the small fish for bait, simply keeping them in a tin with some seaweed to keep them moist. As always, I was loathe to try them when the wrasse of Peninnis Head were so obliging with the hardback crab, but there came a lull in the catch rate, that demanded something of an experiment. A small goby was lip hooked on my paternoster rig and dropped to the bottom. Before I could even lay the rod down I had a hammering bite and missed the fish! Rebaiting with another I dropped it back down and held the rod to await results. Suffice to say, I caught a good wrasse of a couple of pounds on each of those baits.

On other occasions when I have tried rock gobies of five inches or longer they have been taken by conger, and not just strap conger of three pounds, but big eels up into double figures. Even though a mackerel head or fillet is the preferred bait of conger fishermen, it does seem logical to assume that an eel, being a bottom feeder, comes across a whole lot more gobies and blennies, than it does

Small Fish

fast-swimming mackerel.

Catching these small fish is an art in itself. The normal way is to drop-net them, or approach with a prawn net. The latter is something of a loser's game as the fish have an infuriating habit of getting into the exact crack you can't get to with the net. In high summer I have actually caught them using 1-lb line with a freshwater size 20 hook baited with the tiniest piece of mussel or limpet I could cut. It is amazing how cagey they become after you catch a few of their companions and they really deserve a fate better than becoming the bait for a larger fish.

One word of warning. In rock pools that always have some water you are safe, but grubbing around under big rocks and kelp, particularly if there are broken rocks with sand patches, you run the risk of a weaver encounter. This little fish is unlikely to be in the rocky areas, but if you grab hold of one and it injects you with poison from one of its three dorsal spines, you will find yourself in excruciating pain, with a hand swelling like a football, and a long way from a hospital! A simple precaution is to wear a pair of old garden gloves, the type with the coarse inner palms and fingers that prevent thorns penetrating. Remember to wash them in fresh water after each collecting session though, otherwise the salt will rot the material. Check with your identification book so you know what a weaver looks like.

Blennies, gobies and other assorted rock pool fish are not high on my list of sea baits, but nevertheless I feel they should be mentioned as they will often produce good fish.

Sprats

This small pelagic fish is one of the more important in the food chain, as it travels in large shoals, relying on its lateral line to detect subtle pressure changes in the water surrounding it. This is why, when you see a shoal of fish playing 'follow the leader', they change direction almost as one body, and in unison with the lead fish. They are classed as a cold water fish as their primary feeding ground is the rich planktonic areas of the Baltic Sea and waters from Norway right up to the Arctic Seas. A great many anglers think the sprat is a young herring, but it is in fact a totally separate species.

The Thames estuary sees a massive influx of this fish sometime between early December and mid January. Prior to this migration of baitfish the cod fishing is quite good, but once such a huge bulk of food moves into an area, the cod go off all other feed and gorge themselves on the sprat shoals. Some years ago it was nothing to hear commercial netsmen say they hauled in so many their nets burst—or that there were so many in the sea they were being chopped up by the boat's propellers!

The sprat cannot be caught by rod and line, but anglers living near their feeding areas can get superb baits in the shape of fresh sprats when they are brought in to be boxed and sold. The sheen on a fresh sprat is nothing like the dull lack-lustre one you see on a fishmonger's slab, but since the slab is where most anglers are going to get their sprats from, here is a word of advice about buying and using them.

A Tuesday is a good day to buy your bait as this will have given the fishmonger time to buy his new week's stock. If not sold the first day they are kept in a cold store. Obviously the longer they are kept, the softer they go, so try to buy a pound or so of sprats on a Tuesday and freeze them down straight away in readiness for the weekend.

They are best used from the boat and are too soft to stand the rigours of beachcasting. The exception to this rule is when fishing for whiting. This toothy relative of the cod comes in close to shore during winter months and is not averse to taking a fish bait. For that reason, and only provided your sprat is fresh, I suggest a side fillet is taken off with a very sharp knife and then folded double, leaving the scales on the outside. Then hook it through just twice, you can always tie these small fillets to the shank with elasticated cotton, if necessary.

Sprats

Strange as it may seem, it's rare to get a codling on this bait, even though they gorge themselves on sprats in the deeper water.

Whole sprats are best used when you are boat fishing, and then you drop down a single bait on a running leger rig. They are relatively small and you can strike straight away to avoid deep hooking any fish. A good idea is to add some pilchard oil to the bait before you drop it down. Even though it appears the oil washes off on the surface, enough remains to aid the fish to locate the source of smell. In clear water, a couple of sprats fished on loose paternosters over, or near a wreck, work as flashers, taking cod and pollock. I have also heard of a similar method being used off Beachy Head in Sussex for the bass which work over the rocks during late spring and early summer, harassing the whitebait shoals.

Sprats should alway be used as a standby bait.

Sandeels

If peeler crabs are the best bait for the shore angler, then the humble sandeel must be the best for the boat angler. Of course mackerel will run a close second, but a whole mackerel is not a staple diet item for most species, whereas the smaller sandeel is. Many species eat them as they swim freely through the different water levels, feeding on tiny organisms. Think of sandeel and many anglers think of bass, for this species more than any other is synonymous with this bait. Even for the bass, however, the difference in catch rates between live and dead sandeels can be considerable.

This was illustrated to me down in the west country at the port of Dartmouth. Just out from the estuary mouth there is a bank where at certain stages of tide the bass roam. Everybody knows about it of course, so the mark gets a lot of hammering both from professional charter boats and private boats. Nevertheless, while drifting from a charter boat using dead sandeels we took a few bass. I thought this was quite normal, until I saw another boat with a group of anglers using live sandeels with, at one stage, three out of four rods hooped over in a fighting curve.

Another species that likes live eels better is the pollock. During my many years' apprenticeship spent on the Looe boats reef and shark fishing, I learned a lot about pollock. The skipper I was apprenticed to was Alan Dingle, and the boat the *Lady Betty*. Many were the days I came back from famous rocks like the Hands Deeps and Hat Rock with several boxes of pollock. Most times we had more than the other charter boats, simply because of Alan's intimate knowledge of the tides and rocks. He recounted how one day he landed a record 54 stone of pollock (that's over 750 lb), with just one angler on his boat. The bait was of course, a live sandeel fished on a long flowing trace in true west-country fashion.

The sandeel of course, is not really an eel. These long, slim wriggly fish, silvery and with a hint of green on the back, often burrow into the sand to escape other predators. There are two types of interest to the angler: the Lesser Sandeel, and the Greater Sandeel. As you would expect, the only difference between them is size; from a fisherman's point of view they make small baits or big baits.

They are shoal fish, having a large projecting lower jaw, which can

Sandeels

To the bass and pollock angler these are like platinum. Live sandeels kept in a wooden courge are just about the best bait you can use in high summer and clear water conditions.

telescope out to make a transparent scoop. They feed on whitebait, or virtually anything else they can get inside that large-hinged jaw; their dorsal fin runs almost the entire length of the back. Even now, their full life cycle is not entirely understood. In some places they are sought not only as a good multi-species bait, but for eating as well. The Lesser Sandeel will grow to a length of perhaps seven inches, and is most abundant in great shoals around our inshore waters during the summer months. Their preferred habitat is a large sandy estuary, free from pollution. The Greater Sandeel is perhaps not so prolific as the Lesser, and grows to an average of twelve inches in length although I have heard of a Greater Sandeel of 18 inches being caught! In the deep waters off the coast of Scotland there are believed to be

Sea Fishing Baits

two other sandeel species, but they are found in depths that would not be practical for anglers.

There are several ways to procure this bait. They have a habit of living just underneath the sand at low tide, using that extended lower jaw to wriggle quickly out of sight. In some areas it is possible to dig them with a fork, and occasionally you come across a few while digging lugworm. This is a haphazard way to find them however, for no sooner have you dug them up than they wriggle out of sight again. They are so fast they are like quicksilver. The generally accepted method of getting them out and into your bait bucket under these circumstances is to rake them. This is done by an improvised hook or sickle-shaped, blunt blade that is swept around in long easy movements just underneath the sand. This disturbs the sandeels and they wriggle away frantically trying to get back under the sand. You get very little time to grab them, but it is at least a little more productive than using a fork. It is something of an art, and it will take some practise before you can rake sandeels successfully.

I have heard of another method used during the autumn months when low spring tides coincide with midnight, and they can be collected by torchlight. I have been around and about many times at midnight on a beach, but I confess to never having seen any sandeels being lured into the lamplight! I would think this occurrence is somewhat rare, and most probably confined to certain areas of estuary and beach.

Here are two other ways to collect sandeels. One is to buy them frozen from the tackle shop. Invariably they will have been blast frozen while fresh, and still be good enough for using on the beach or boat. I have to say that I have never had much success using them for bass, and I prefer to freeze them fresh myself after dipping them in a pilchard oil and salt mix. This toughens them up a bit, and also gives them a better smell when you get them out of the freezer. Frozen sandeels are a convenience bait for those who cannot get near the sea at the best time to collect them.

The other way to get hold of them is by buying them live from the commercial bait netters who operate on several west-country rivers. They work mostly in the spring to autumn period using a large seine

If you want to get a really good catch like this shared by two anglers in a dinghy off the Kent coast, put plenty of those lugworm on the hook and up the line.

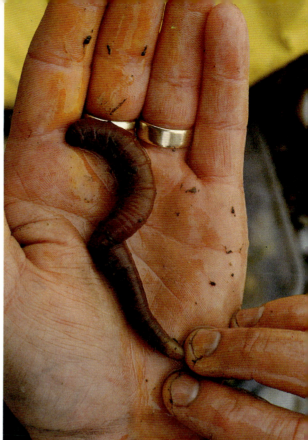

Facing page: While digging black lugworm requires a long narrow spade with worms dug individually, ordinary blow lugworm can be trench dug, especially when the casts are as thick as those shown here.

Inset: Prime fresh lugworm like these are best fished with all their juices in, so avoid squeezing the guts out, unless you intend to roll them in clean newspaper to keep them a couple of days.

Above left: As mackerel is the most popular boat angler's bait, then the humble lugworm must fill the same position for shore fishermen. They are a soft bait with a high water content in their body. Use only fine wire hooks to avoid damaging the bait too much.

Above right: A single lugworm is good for most shore species, but for cod you may need to thread two or three up the line, as after casting you lose a lot of those important body juices and have a small bait.

Right: With lugworm you need to damage the body juices as little as possible. For that reason use fine wire hooks, even if you have to mount them in tandem to stop the worm sliding down to the bend of the hook.

Above left: This rare photograph shows the difference between the red ragworm that will not spawn (left), and the contrasting green ragworm, which is beginning to 'milk up' with eggs, and will be too soft for bait.

Above right: These are 'White Gold', the most precious bait to shore match anglers. Also referred to as 'snakes', the white ragworm can be kept alive in an aerated bucket of water for use as a premier flatfish and cod bait when the going gets tough.

Left: When papered off and kept in dry silver sand, these ragworm will last several days if kept in a cool place. That way you can use them when conditions are best.

Facing page: This is the freshest squid you can get. The author took this two-foot-long specimen as it grabbed his set of flasher feathers off Hook Head in Co. Wexford, Ireland. This would have been superb for eating, but it ended up being cut into strips and dropped back down for other species.

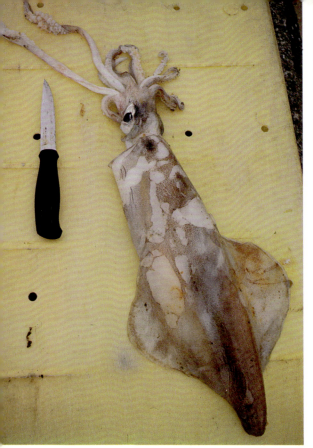

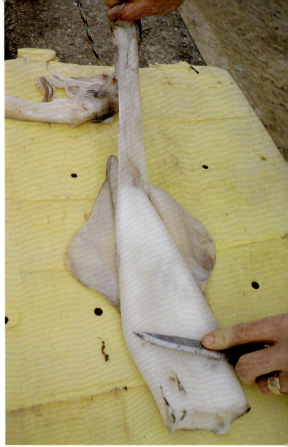

Above left: To prepare a squid for baits, first wash out the ink that will be inside the body cavity.

Left: Remove the head and main guts by pinning the head down using the knife and pulling the body away.

Left: The guts and head should come free quite easily.

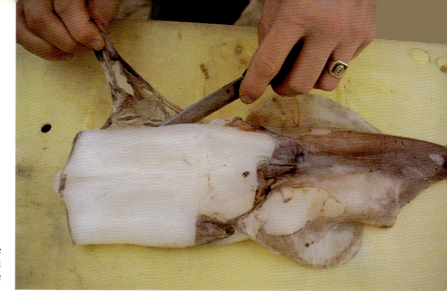

Right: Carefully peel off the darker skin which is like wet cling film, this reveals the pure white meat beneath.

Facing page: Peel this skin completely off the body, and discard. It is useless as bait.

Right: Lay the squid body flat and make an incision the length of the body.

Right: This allows you to open the body up and scrape out the skeleton, which is like a clear piece of plastic, and any remaining guts.

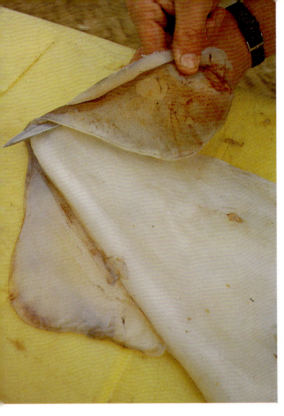 

Cut off the flanges known as the wings. Some anglers use these as bait, but I personally throw them away as being too thin.

You can then fold the entire body out like a piece of cloth and cut the meat into whatever sized strips you want.

Durability is the key word to squid as a fishing bait. Even small strips of squid are devoured avidly by small fish.

Sandeels

net with a fine mesh worked from a rowing boat. Either an open sandy surf beach or estuary is netted, and under good conditions during spring tides, a huge haul of sandeels is made. They are kept alive until sale by placing them in a large wooden courge or penner. This is basically a triangular wooden box with small holes drilled into it to allow seawater to circulate to the occupants. The triangular shape makes it stable when it is moored out in the tide—obviously above the low water line, so it doesn't dry out. The eels can be kept like this for long periods.

There are a few tackle shops that will sell them live to you, having their own tank of seawater at the shop, but generally it is better to buy a couple of pounds' worth from the commercial netter, and transport them home in a box of wet seaweed. They last a few hours if kept wet. From here you can keep them in a normal aquarium of seawater, but you must have it fitted with a proper aeration system. Sandeels need oxygen, and will last a long time provided there is a high oxygen saturation level in the tank.

When you want to take them on the next boat trip or on a beach session, take a plastic bucket with holes punched in the lid and a slot cut for taking a battery-powered aeration pump (available from most tackle shops). If the batteries are the copper-coloured top ones, it should be possible to keep the bait alive for a full day's (or night's) fishing, and you can always bring them back home and keep them in the tank. If any die, take them out and throw them away as their decaying flesh will kill the other live ones.

Sandeels, although appearing tough and resilient, are quite delicate for most hooks. I suggest just hooking lightly either once through the tail, or the standard, 'in the mouth, out the lower jaw, and in through the pectorals' routine. Again, keep your hookholds as light as possible. Even when floatfishing them from the rocks, you must ensure the eel's gills are not restricted by the shank of the hook or they will stop breathing and die. This is why you pull the hookpoint through the lower membrane of the hinged extending lower jaw, so there will be no restriction on the flow of seawater through the gills.

Small live sandeels make excellent baits for flatfish, but if you have to distance cast with them from the beach you will almost certainly

Sea Fishing Baits

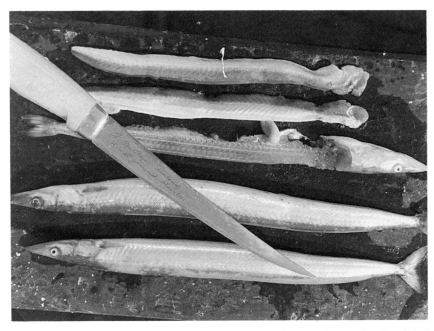

The Greater Sandeel or Launce is better with two fillets taken from the flanks rather than fished whole. Excellent for big plaice, turbot and brill.

need a freshly killed one. The hookpoint must go in near the tail, leaving an inch or so of space, then having bent the eel bring the hook out near the head. The bait will then be hanging upside down. To stop the bait spinning in the air during the cast, you tie the tail root to your main snood and the hookbait can then be used in conjunction with a baitclip. This rig is ideal for all the species of big rays, including turbot.

Some anglers swear by a method of preserving the sandeels in a formalin mixture which toughens them up for this distance casting. They may stay on the hook better, but there is definitely something suspect about such preserved baits, and I feel the formalin kills any natural smells that might attract the predators.

The lesser sandeel is a first-class bait to use, albeit a bit finicky to keep alive. However once you have experienced the voracious manner in which they are devoured by many species, you will think

Sandeels

time spent keeping the eel alive, is time well spent.

Sandeels are one of the most important links in the marine food chain, and provides a meal for nearly every fish we have around our coastline. Their safety from natural predators lies in their numbers, as they swim in vast schools, but this leaves them open to the ravages of commercial over-exploitation. In the North Sea they are fished commercially by Denmark who have landed up to 400,000 tons for processing, and Germany who have landed up to 20,000 tons.

The Greater Sandeel is usually too large to be used as a single hookbait, and is not so prolific as the Lesser Sandeel. They are very predatory and are taken by anglers fishing for mackerel using 'flasher'-type feathers when they are foulhooked as they try to grab the flashing feathers, which I assume they mistake for whitebait. They spawn in the North Sea sometime between April and August, and the eggs hatch in just two to three weeks. Even after they have spawned, sandeels will still eat their own young.

I have heard of some Greater Sandeels (often called Lance or Launce), being used whole for big pollock on the drift, or big turbot at anchor near a wreck. While this may sometimes be successful, I think you would do better to take two long, thin fillets off using a very sharp filleting knife. That way you can get two baits from one fish, but remember the fillet will be very thin, and will be no good for beachcasting. Invariably the Greater Sandeel is taken by boat anglers, so rig with either a tandem double-hook rig to hold the fillet in a straight line, or bind the fillet near the eye of the hook using elasticated cotton. I prefer the double hook rig, as you often get cases of big flatfish plucking at the hookless fluttering end of the fillet, away from the hook. By using a two-hook rig, you can slide the fillet up over the main hook and tag it out straight by the retaining hook. Even a 'nibbler' should then have one of the hooks in its mouth.

As a point of interest, I recently heard of long fillets from Greater Sandeels being dyed with the coloured dyes available for freshwater carp anglers. Apparently this is good for pollock fishing on a drifting boat, and can be deadly at anchor in a strong tide. I have some misgivings about this myself, but by all means experiment. I still feel you will have to go a long way to beat a live sandeel.

Herring

The plankton-rich waters of the Arctic and North Sea have meant the herring is one of our most prolific baitfish. It was fished very heavily during the early 1950s, by drift-netters operating in the North Sea but they were too successful, and the species reached the verge of extinction. This cost the British angler the only real chance he had of catching the strongest fish in the world—the Bluefin Tuna. These were caught by a few pioneering anglers in the war years and in the early 1950s, when the fish moved in close around the drift netters as they hauled their catch from the water at dawn after drifting through the night. Huge Bluefin tuna in excess of 700 lb fed heavily on the net spillage, and therefore represented a viable possibility to hardy anglers. Alas, with the almost suicidal tendencies of commercial fishermen taking so many herring, the Bluefin disappeared, and today, although the herring has returned following a ban on its fishing, the Bluefin has not. I personally feel there will never be a Bluefin landed now in excess of 800 lb; the only place I can think of where it might happen is the west coast of Ireland, where they have located Bluefins feeding on scad and mackerel shoals.

Herrings move in vast shoals using sound waves to follow-the-leader, and move almost as one body. This makes a huge shoal an easy target for a netsman kitted out with all the very latest in electronic fish locators. As an important food, much research has gone into finding out about the herring's movements, its growth and spawning. A soft-finned fish, with a beautiful opalescent green-blue back, the herring has plenty of oil in its flesh to make it a good bait. Each female can lay up to 30,000 eggs, which makes the roe a popular food both with humans and fish.

Young herrings move to shallow water from the deep, often into estuaries, and have even been known to move as far up the Thames as Blackwall. From here they go back out to deeper water (where they go to nobody seems to know) and then come back as mature adults. They are rarely caught on rod and line because of their tiny mouths but I have seen them caught off Southend pier by youngsters in the winter, floatfishing tiny pieces of worm on freshwater hooks.

The best herrings are purchased from a netter docking with a haul of this silvery baitfish. Only then does the colour and remarkable

Herring

Never underestimate the power of these jaws. Although toothless, the jaws on a conger have phenomenal gripping power, which coupled to that muscular body, mean unhooking should be carefully done. They respond well to mackerel, herring, squid and pouting.

sheen stay on the fish's flanks. You can buy them from the fishmonger's slab, and they will work well in deep water from the boat for a wide variety of species like skate, tope, dogfish, spurdog, ling and conger. But once you have seen a fresh one, unfrozen, you realise that those found on the fishmonger's slab are poor in comparison.

The best way to fish this bait whole is by threading it up the hook using a baiting needle to avoid splitting the meat open. Fished whole, they are great for tope, conger, cod and skate. You can also take cross-sections of the whole fish using a sharp filleting knife and use

Sea Fishing Baits

them as what the Americans call 'chunk-baits'. The flanks can also be filleted off, and make a good all-round sized bait for most species especially skate and rays. Place a fillet on the hook only once, do not thread it up the shank otherwise the tide action will fold it down into the bend of the hook, making an unattractive ball. You can get round this by using elasticated cotton, and tying the fillet to the trace, above the hook eye. Better just to nick it on once though, and simply give any subsequent bite you get, a little bit longer so the hook is inside the mouth.

If you do take both side fillets off as a bait, remember not to throw the head and guts away, as for conger and the bigger thornback skate, this is the best bit. Full of blood, juice and oils, its scent is trickled downtide to attract the larger predators.

Use frozen or shop-bought herring if you have no alternative, but if you get the chance to buy them fresh, do so. Buy as large a quantity as you can, and freeze them down yourself into smaller day-size bait packs.

Smelt

I have no idea where most fish get their names from, but the smelt must surely get its name from its smell. Much like the grayling of our freshwater rivers, the smelt has a distinctive cucumber scent—so much so that years ago when they were taken commercially, they were referred to as 'cucumber fish'.

Also known as the sparling, this little fish was once thought to live only in estuaries, in muddy holes on the bottom. It only grows to about eight inches, and an average fish would be about five inches. Smelt are at their most prolific during the winter months from September to May, when they shoal up for spawning. It will not be caught except by accident on a rod and line. The only live one I ever saw was when a friend, Jerry Airey from Essex, took one while we were floatfishing tiny pieces of ragworm in the sewer outfall at Hope Cove in Devon. Not the best place to fish as far as scents go, but it amused us to catch a 'smelt' from a venue that definitely 'smelt'!

They make an excellent deadbait for pike fishing in freshwater, where they are fished as a whole fish. I know of no commercial fisheries you can buy them from except maybe from the sprat fishermen operating in the Thames estuary during winter.

A durable fish, you can get them from the fishmongers, and use them either as 'chunkbait' or fish them whole. The beauty of them is that they are certainly different, and fished whole on a long flowing trace are good for thornback skate and bass. Coat them with pilchard oil though as their natural cucumber scent isn't particularly attractive to a predator.

Pilchards

Although I'm told pilchards can grow to about nine inches, I have never seen one even approaching that size. They are common off the Spanish and French coast where they are an important item both in the marine food chain, and also as a food for humans. They were also once prolific off the Cornish coast. An incredibly oily fish, they were responsible for tremendous blue shark catches some thirty years ago in Cornwall. In fact, at the Cornish port of Looe, there used to be a pilchard canning factory in operation. When all the wastage from the canning factory ran into the river the bass, pollock and flounder fishing was amazing. Since the closure of the factory many years ago, the fishing has declined dramatically.

This fish spawns throughout the whole of the English Channel, on up into the North Sea, and contains a very high oil content. When bought fresh from a trawler they are an excellent bait, especially when fillets are taken from each flank. Their bad point is that they deteriorate very quickly because of the high oil content in the flesh.

If I had to choose a top bait for conger, it would be the pilchard and because of their high oil content there is no need to use any other additive; they send up a slick all on their own.

A tip worth noting in case you fancy an odd day out sharking is to mix pilchard oil with bran. On one particular sharking expedition in the Isles of Scilly, after struggling to get enough mackerel for a chum slick, I went into the local supermarket and bought a dozen cans of pilchards in oil! If I recall correctly we caught three blues that day.

You will no doubt have noticed throughout this book that I have a fondness for mixing any baits, or at least coating them with pilchard oil. It has seen me outfish other anglers so many times I cannot understand why more anglers don't use it. I buy a gallon can of pilchard oil concentrate from Brent's of Hailsham in Sussex, and then bottle it down to suit my own requirements: 500-ml bottles for sharking trips where I mix it in the chum or rubby dubby, or smaller squeezy bottles with a nozzle for anointing individual baits. In my view the humble pilchard beats the hell out of many of the fancy 'magic' additives now on sale.

Pouting and Poor Cod

I have already talked about the advantage of using small fish as bait for larger predators when I spoke of blennies and rock gobies used from the shore. All fish prey either on each other or on other species at some time or other and this is why they should be considered for bait.

Two species that the boat angler may come into contact with when fishing deep water using small hooks are the pouting and 'poor' cod. Invariably they will be caught as a by-product of intent on worthier specimens, but don't discard them, for it is these little fish that could put you in contact with the big fish. They should be of particular interest to the conger eel angler, as both the poor cod and pouting frequent the eel's habitat, and are therefore at the top of its food list. The pouting especially is a prime food for the big eels, so anything from 1 lb in weight downwards should be kept for hookbait.

Big pouting over 3 lb are good little scrappers provided you scale down your tackle accordingly, but half pound to $1^{1}/_{4}$ lb fish are ideal eel baits. If you are out over a wreck intent on catching only big conger of 30 to 50 lb, then rig a whole 1-lb pouting on a short running leger, and drop it down to await results. If you are reef or rough-ground fishing, where the average conger will possibly break into double figures, then use half-pound pouting. Remember to mount them in such a way that the hookpoint is near the head, as invariably a conger will swallow it head first. Should you be picking up pouting in shallow depths, then wind them to the surface slowly to prevent them 'blowing' with the air pressure as they rise and when you lip-hook them, drop them back down, equally as slowly, to fish as a livebait. In deep water they always come up goggle-eyed with the change in depth, but if you get them from shallow water it means you can use them live. On very big pouting of up to 2 lb apiece, take a whole fillet off each side using a razor sharp filleting knife. Then place the two fillets side by side before running the hook through them just once. This is the original flapper bait that wobbles around in the tide and attracts the eels.

Occasionally you will catch the poor cod, which rarely exceeds eight inches in length, and is a brownish-yellow colour on the back. Many anglers feel they are just small pouting, but they are indeed a

Sea Fishing Baits

This youngster looks well pleased with his brace of big pouting, and while fun to a youngster using a light rod, they represent a primary food source for huge wreck conger over 50lb in weight. This size pouting would fish best as fillets.

Pouting and Poor Cod

separate species, and travel inshore to feed on shrimps. Both pouting and the poor cod have a habit of going 'off' really quickly, and I would advise using both of these baits on the same day you catch them. They can be kept a bit fresher if you place them in a bucket of seawater and put them in the shade until you use them. They are hardly worth eating yourself, and only seem edible when somebody goes to the trouble of turning them into fish cakes. I feel they are better suited to baits and would use the bigger pouting as conger bait in the summer and autumn, and the poor cod as a good winter bait for its larger cousin, the true cod.

Mackerel

Without a doubt this is the boat angler's premier baitfish, forming as it does, an integral link in the food chain. The mackerel, when fished for with light tackle is one of the hardest fighters you can find in British waters; it's just unfortunate that they don't grow to double figures! They are shoal fish, very fast swimmers, and almost constantly on the lookout for food; much like that big-game fish the tuna. Both have extra blood in their tissues which not only gives them incredible vigour, but also makes them about the best bait you can get for almost any other fish. I doubt there are many fish that catch and eat a fleeting mackerel, but when they are preoccupied with either feeding on sandeels and whitebait, or spawning, they will be eaten by sharks, tope and occasionally bass. Bottom fish have no chance of catching one, but even so they fully appreciate that blood-rich meat when it is dangled in front of them.

There is little point in putting any additives on the mackerel as its blood and oil content is so high already. Mackerel are good to eat when cooked fresh but most get ground up for fish meal. The vast shoals approach our British shoreline in late spring, and depart from inshore waters in late autumn. They are migratory, and thanks to modern electronic fish-finding equipment they are facing virtual extinction at the hands of the commercial fisheries.

When spawning shoals were located off the Lizard peninsula in Cornwall, fantastic hauls of fish were taken, with entire schools being wiped out in one sweep of the net; indeed some trawlers had nets so full they had to cut them away to prevent sinking! Eventually catch quotas were introduced to protect them but already the commercials are reaching their quotas almost immediately. A female mackerel can lay up to half a million eggs, so it is easy to imagine the damage being done to future generations when thousands of tons of spawning females are taken.

It is possible to purchase mackerel from the fishmonger, and some tackle dealers also keep a supply frozen down, but it is always best to use them fresh whenever possible. The problem with deep freezing any fish for a length of time is that it dehydrates it and the skin tends to split. Underneath, the flesh will be pappy and soft, grey in colour, and useful only for bait on spurdogs. If you can catch them and

Mackerel

freeze them in a few hours they retain some of their colours and are a better bait, but once thawed out properly they still go soft and break up. Catching fresh mackerel couldn't be easier technically—you simply drop down a set of mackerel feathers and jig them up and down to imitate whitebait or sandeels. The main difficulty is in actually finding them. Look for banks, rock pinnacles or tide races or any other feature that may indicate food. Usually they are found by the boat's echo sounder, and can be anywhere from right on the surface to down near the bottom, even in fifty fathoms of water—but the drawback to the echo sounder is that of course many shoal fish such as sprats and herring will give the same sounder reading as a shoal of mackerel.

While some mackerel can be taken by towing a small, heavily-weighted spinner behind a boat, this is an impractical method for getting a bait supply. Jigging on the other hand is so simple a five-year-old could do it. Here are a few tips that I use to locate them, and catch them quicker. After all, the quicker you catch them, the quicker you can start fishing. I have sometimes spent half a day looking for bait, and I don't doubt that at some time or other every angler has experienced this frustration. So—to catch mackerel I use a heavy lead. You can use a light three or four ounce lead for your weight, but in my experience I have found this sinks too slowly. The mackerel is a very fast-feeding predator and he is more likely to hit something that flashes quickly, so the two main reasons I use a heavy lead is firstly that it gets down quickly, which allows me to search out the correct depth or layer quickly, and secondly two that it goes down so quickly that it invariably snags into a school of mackerel, and foulhooks one. This stops the lead instantly at exactly the right depth the shoal is feeding at. Often other mackerel will quickly snatch at the feathers and you get a full string of bait, or what is known as a 'full house'. I leave my flashers down longer than most anglers in an effort to get other mackerel to fill up the remaining feathers. A word of warning when doing this though: when you first hit that single fish, and you leave the flashers down a few seconds to fill up, ensure you keep a tight line.

On no account let the line fall slack otherwise the fish will swim

Sea Fishing Baits

around, tangling the snoods, and leaving them in a terrible mess—which means you then have to waste valuable fishing time untangling it all. No—what I do is this. I take the reel out of gear and let the lead plummet away for twenty feet before stopping the spool with my thumb and sweeping the rod upwards. I then release the spool and let another twenty feet run down, repeating the procedure. This way I search the layers every twenty feet until I find them, but usually they will stop the lead themselves on the way down.

Take care when you swing a string of mackerel aboard for unhooking. Grab the lead at the bottom and hold the rod horizontally, leaving them dangling like a washing line. Then you can either unhook them yourself, or get someone to do it for you.

If you only have a couple of mackerel on a six-hook trace beware the loose snoods. More accidents occur with mackerel feathers than any other terminal rig, and the barb on a mackerel hook is fairly basic to say the least. I've yet to see the angler who has the courage to rip a mackerel hook out that is embedded past the barb, in the same manner as he unhooks a dogfish! An easy method of unhooking is to hold the hookshank hard and shake them off. Like many species of tuna, the mackerel has a fairly soft mouth which tears quite easily. Don't leave fish flapping all over the place so they end up down the bilges. Put them in the bait box, and on a sunny day, keep it in the shade. A good method in hot weather is to put a dozen in a bucket of seawater placed in the shade, or at least covered with a piece of wet rag or towelling. If you use those last, they will still be fresh.

As for catching mackerel from the shore, this can be done with feathers or flashers, but is far more enjoyable on a light spinning rod. Many small artificials represent whitebait or sandeels and are successful mostly during the hours of low light conditions, at dawn or dusk. If you use one of the heavier casting spoons like the Ryobi Odin lure, try a couple of retrieves fairly fast over the surface. Then allow it to flutter deeper, about twelve feet down and retrieve in long sweeps. The darker it gets, the higher in the surface layers the fish rise, so don't forget a few last casts across the surface. Mackerel can also be taken by floatfishing a tiny piece of fish strip on the edge of a tide run, or even freelining a small frozen sandeel. You will find that

Mackerel

The 'Split-tail' mackerel as popularised by the author on his tope fishing expeditions.

catching them from the shore is a lot more satisfying than from a boat, and gives you more respect for each fish caught.

As for types of bait you can use mackerel for, the list is almost endless. Here's an unusual tip that I bet hardly any of you know. One of the best mullet baits, and I've never written of this before, is to use a piece of gut and stomach lining from the mackerel. With mullet being such a finicky feeder it is often difficult to imitate the exact food it is feeding on. However mackerel feed on tiny crustaceans and their stomach lining and wall will have a strong smell of this which attracts mullet. A small tip, but it may help you catch that extra picky mullet.

The best cut of mackerel is the flank, otherwise known as a fillet. This is a long cut made from just behind the gill. Stroke the filleting knife down the edge of the backbone and bring the blade out near the tail. A whole large fillet like this can be used for big fish like skate, tope, shark and conger. By laying the fillet skin-side down on the cutting board you can either split it straight down the centre to make

Sea Fishing Baits

two long thin strips, or cut it diagonally to make maybe five cross-cut small baits. With five cross-cut baits from each fillet you have eleven baits, because you still have the head and guts left over. Do not simply throw these overboard unless you are intentionally groundbaiting. They are most effective for conger, big bull huss and ling, when fished hard on the bottom, hook once through both eye sockets.

But before you get this far, let's go back to the stage where you have removed both flank fillets. Attached to the main skeleton you should have a thin white strip of belly meat attached from the throat to the tail. This is very narrow and is perfect for use as a turbot bait, presumably because it can bend and waver in the tidal currents like a sandeel or launce. Remove this simply by nicking the place where it is attached with the filleting knife. Put the hook point through it twice near the thickest end, and it will waver about properly. Put the hook through too many times and it will simply bunch up in an unattractive heap in the bend, and catch nothing.

The presentation of any sea bait is just as important as the acquisition and cutting of it. Remember to use only the sharpest knife (the Normark filleting knife is one of the best), and keep it sharpened on a fine carborundum stone. Rinse with water after each use to get rid of any ground-up residue. Do not on any account leave your razor-sharp filleting knife lying around on the deck. Better to place it back in the sheath, or slide the blade under the edge of the bait board so nobody can slip and cut themselves on it. Some bait boards resemble an explosion at an abattoir. Such a mess on the board gets in the way of the next bait preparation, so knock the contents into the water, and dunk the board in a few times to wash it off. That extra smell in the water does no harm, and you'll have a clean board for the next lot of bait.

Now I have to make a confession. I stated earlier that there is really no need to put any additive onto a fresh fillet of mackerel. Well—I admit that I always anoint even my own fresh fillets with some of that Brent's pilchard oil. It's more force of habit than anything else, but I am so accustomed to using the stuff it's a wonder I don't put it on my chips!

Don't lose your squid head! The author swings in a strap conger taken from the shore on a whole squid head.

A whole Calamari squid mounted on a double hook rig is one of the best bottom fishing baits for the big cod like this twenty pounder taken by the author.

Conger feed well on whole squid, although they must seldom get the chance to feed on them in their natural state.

A cousin to the squid is the cuttlefish, the dried skeleton of which usually finds its way into the budgie's cage. Cuttlefish is, if anything, even tougher than squid and makes a great bait that can be used to catch more than one fish.

One of the more exotic baits is the octopus. Treat it the same as squid, but personally I reckon they are better to eat yourself than feed to the fish!

Possibly the finest bait for a specimen fish—the crab can be found all around our coastline, and favours kelp-covered rocks and boulders.

This rare shot shows a male crab carrying the female underneath him for mating. The female will have the softer shell and makes the better bait.

Author Graeme Pullen swings in another shore fish, taken on peeler crab during a session after a big shore bass. The best bait often produces the better fish.

Mackerel

Mackerel cubes and mackerel meal. Mixed together and thrown over as groundbait, they will attract a variety of fish.

Another tip, which you can either make use of or discard, but which works well for me, is to use cubes of mackerel flesh for groundbait or 'chum' to bring various species on the feed. I only do this when I have a steady supply of baits, but I have gutted many ground fish like conger, cod and even black bream, that have had cubes of mackerel in them, so I know it works well. Nobody ever uses cubes for bait. Also you may be able to get your local tackle dealer to get you some mackerel meal. This is a powdered sort of fish meal, that can mix into a good groundbait, and can be thrown into the swim to attract predators. I have used it to good effect in the shallow bay waters of Ireland, and had good results with tope and monkfish.

Mackerel is surely our main baitfish, and I hope that in the future its harvesting commercially as a food source is managed correctly. It's easy to get greedy and overfish them—even as an individual angler—so take only those that you need for bait.

Lugworm

What the maggot is to the freshwater fisherman, so the lugworm is to the sea fisherman. This is probably the British sea angler's most popular bait, certainly as far as shore fishing is concerned. On a national basis lugworm can be dug easily from most beaches, although in recent years we have seen a restriction put on some wildlife sanctuaries, where digging is thought to be detrimental to the other wildlife. I cannot see how this would be possible, as most birds don't dig up worms from eighteen inches below the surface, but I know that occasionally whole areas have been dug dry by over-enthusiastic commercial bait diggers. Still—as it's the anglers that create the demand, I suppose we must shoulder some of the responsibility, and the more popular fishing becomes the more worms will be needed to satisfy that demand.

The lug is a burrowing worm that betrays its presence to the avid bait collector by the pile of sand it leaves on the surface. There may also be a slight depression a few inches from the sand pile. To get them out dig down between the depression and pile and you should locate them. They lie in a U-shaped burrow, where after swallowing some sand, they extract their food and deposit the unwanted grains on the surface, thus forming the pile. The front and middle sections of a lugworm are much thicker than the tail section, the tail being the part with the least juice in.

There are two types of lug that will interest the angler: the blow lug, and the black lug. Both are excellent fish catchers, due to the attractant qualities of the amino acids in their body juices. Many artificial additives and worms have been manufactured in an effort to duplicate these but up to now none of them has really proved to be better than the real thing.

Blow lug can be dug around much of the British Isles, but are more popular along the east coast of England, where their primary use is in the capture of cod during the winter months. Having said that, lug will be taken by every member of the flatfish family, all the cod family, and even some of the predators like pollock and conger. The main drawback with blow lug is that their water content is very high. They are at best a soft bait, and care must be taken during both digging and storage. The black lug is a whole lot tougher but requires

Lugworm

a different digging technique—but let's deal with the blow lug first.

Many tackle shops will supply blow lugs and they can be purchased by either quantity, i.e. so much per 100, or by weight, i.e. so much per lb. Given a choice it is better to buy them by number, as you can occasionally be cheated by diggers who put too much sand in with the worms.

As for digging them yourself, first you must look for a good sand or mudflat. The lug casts, by which they are located, can be found about mid-way down the ebb tide line, but the bigger and more prolific worm beds will be nearer the low tide mark. Also remember a spring tide goes out farther on its low tide mark. On open flat sandy beaches where the tide goes out a long way you may have to take into account the remaining surface water on the sand, which will make individual worm digging difficult and then it may be better to trench dig them. This is best done in an area where the number of worm casts are most plentiful. Start by taking several spits of sand out and stacking them in a line three fork widths across, against the wind. This will stop the surface water from draining into the trench, making it too sloppy to dig and aiding the worm's escape. Then dig a line downwind from your barrier of sand, throwing it out on the sides. Try not to break any worms, but if you do (and it happens a lot), place them in a separate container otherwise the dead worms will contaminate and kill all the live ones.

How many worms you need is decided by many things: the length of your fishing session, species sought, number of rods used, and number of worms you want to keep for the next trip. It's almost impossible to say, but I wouldn't feel happy with much less than eighty blow lug for a session after cod and whiting, stretching to maybe 150 for an all-night and all-day session. Nothing is worse than wastage, especially when you have put so much effort into digging them. Blow lug often only last one cast, and if the quarry is cod and the worms are small, you may have to mount two or three worms on the hook. Should there be any piece of worm left over when you bring your end tackle in, leave it on, sliding it up over the hook eye and up the trace. Then put another worm or two on to give you a larger bait.

The black lug. This is not so readily available as the blow lug, and

Last light and professional black lugworm diggers look for the last few worms before an incoming tide pushes them off the beach. Black lug are much stronger for casting than the softer blow lug.

certainly requires considerable effort to collect. Black lug live much deeper in the sand, often over two feet down, and are spread over a wider area, thus making trench digging impractical. For most worm digging, a flat-pronged potato fork is ideal, but for black-lug digging you need to get down very deep and very fast. For that reason a narrow spade is needed, which cuts a narrow spit straight down to the worm. After locating the cast you need to get three or four spits of sand out quickly, then carefully search the remaining foot of sand for the lug.

Lugworm

There are two schools of thought about what to do when you get to this stage. For years many diggers would 'gut' both the blow lug or the black lug, squeezing out all the sand or mud inside before storing it, but recently many of the top beach matchmen have decided against this, reasoning that the more juice left in the bait, the better it is for drawing bigger fish. The black lug is gutted to make it tougher and to avoid it going soft and watery, but ungutted worms are still tough provided they are stored in paper, and have that body juice in them.

There are several ways to keep your lug, and for black lug the best way is to rinse them in fresh seawater immediately after digging, then once home empty them onto some sheets of newspaper. Roll them gently around so the paper soaks up the excess moisture, then roll each worm individually in a fold of newspaper. Most anglers roll ten worms in one tabloid sheet. Do not use glossy paper, but ordinary newsprint that is absorbent. Kept in a cool place like a garage, or better still a fridge, they will keep for around a week. If your next trip isn't for a couple of weeks, or if you have some black lug left over from a previous trip, you can freeze them down.

Some matchmen just blanch them by quickly scalding them in boiling water, and then freezing them. I haven't tried this myself, but I am assured it does catch fish. My way though is to take a small dish and put in it some table salt and pilchard oil. Take each worm, dip it in the mix, wipe it against the edge of the dish to remove excess oil, and wrap individually. Pack about ten to a sheet of newspaper and freeze them down. These worms definitely catch fish, and of course it means you can go fishing at short notice. Another way is to thread each worm individually on to a hook and length of snood, then freeze these down. This way you can still cast a long way with a partly frozen bait, but it entails using a large number of hooks and snoods, plus I am not at all sure what happens to the structure of the nylon snood when subjected to freezing temperatures. I suspect it may be weakened.

Another way is to thread the worm onto a thin metal spike, almost like a kebab, so that the worm is frozen straight, and can be threaded onto your hook and snood. Several types of wire can be used, the

Sea Fishing Baits

thinner the better. Coat-hanger wire is OK, but thinner wire obtained from model shops for aircraft undercarriages is ideal; SWG 18 gauge is about right, and is also good for making wires for your grip leads. The 'kebab' worms are then rolled in sheets of tin foil or newspaper and frozen in sheets of ten. To take them fishing why not use a cool box like those insulated varieties that allow you to use pre-frozen blocks. A thermos flask can also be used, and this means that if you have worms left over from a fishing trip you can put them back into your stock. This method is good if you intend casting a long way and need a firm bait, plus you can stock up with a supply for the winter hours, when digging worms becomes harder.

If one of the first things to kill lugworm is a dead worm of their own kind, the second thing must surely be an increase in temperature. They simply will not tolerate any warm place, so in the summer months you will have to go to some length to prevent them getting too hot. One way is to put one of the chemical freeze blocks available for picnicking into an old tupperware box. Place a sheet or two of corrugated paper over the top, and then put your worms, still in the newspaper, on the top. Cover with loose newspaper and they should keep a long time, certainly the duration of your trip, but use some common-sense and keep them out of the sun.

The final way to look after those precious worms is to keep them alive in a seawater tank. There is little doubt that a live fresh worm will outfish a frozen one, and if you want a good catch rate it will be in your own interest to keep the lugworm alive. If you use an old aquarium tank, be sure to use only seawater and buy an aeration pump and filter system. Exactly the same as you would for keeping fish, but this time you will have worms! It's better to re-stock your tank on the little-and-often basis, rather than go out and do a back-breaking dig for 200 worms.

Some aeration pumps are reputed to actually warm the seawater in the tank and thereby kill the worms off. This problem can be overcome by freezing down some tupperware containers of seawater, then when frozen, dropping the ice into the tank. This keeps the tank cooler. To get the ice out of the plastic frozen container, tap it out gently first, or run it under the cold tap for a minute. Don't hammer

Lugworm

it or you're likely to smash the brittle container as well. Another way to overcome this temperature change problem is to use several large plastic containers for the worms, instead of the aquarium tank. These smaller containers can be fitted inside an old fridge which can be wired up in the garage, with the air tube from the aerator leading out through a tiny drilled hole, and the actual pump itself kept outside.

Freshwater anglers always use a fridge to keep maggots in, so that their body temperature is kept low to keep them in a slow-moving, almost comatose state, and to prevent them changing into casters. Four gallon-size plastic tanks or containers should be ample for supporting around three hundred worms if you spread the numbers evenly through each container. On no account overstock, otherwise the fatality rate will rise. Whatever you do though, you are bound to lose a few worms in the first week of operation, and in this event take them out and freeze them down using the pilchard oil and old newspaper technique.

Some anglers believe that 'tanked' worms lose those important body juices during their confinement, but I feel this disadvantage is far outweighed by the fact that it keeps the worms alive—and fresh worms are so much better for cod, whiting and flounder than the frozen variety. If you keep a frequent daily check on the worms in the tank, and remove those dead ones, it has been found that a hardy supply of undamaged worms can last for 6 weeks. Even though you have to go to considerable trouble in setting up this operation, it does have the added advantage that you can go fishing at any time with up to 300 fresh, live lugworm whether in the heat of summer or frosts of winter.

Of course you still have that back-breaking task of digging the worms in the first place, and I'm afraid there is no easy way round that. I heard of a commercial worm-digging machine some years ago, but it never did get off the ground, which may not be a bad thing. Can you imagine the look on some birdwatcher's face as he pans the shoreline with his binoculars for a rare species of wading bird, and sees a huge machine throwing sand everywhere as it collects thousands of lugworm? Let's stick to the humble fork, and get those back muscles exercised!

Ragworm

I would rate the ragworm as the second most popular bait among anglers, even though its use may be regionalised because of its availability. There are three similar types of rag: harbour rag, white rag and red rag—and possibly four if you count king ragworm as being different. Personally I feel the king rag is just a large red ragworm, but as I say, many anglers feel they are completely different.

King rag can grow to a size almost too big to use as a single hookbait, and I have seen exceptional specimens used as four ample baits! In fact there is one species, the *Nereis Virens* whose length has been recorded at over three feet. This one is green with a purple back and pink belly and lives in old shells vacated by hermit crabs, and as all ragworm possess pincers, the power of a three-foot-long specimen seems to me downright dangerous. The pincers are a pair of extendable black, needle-sharp nippers that pop out from the thick end of the head. Because of their size, king rag have generated stories around them, like they are supposed to be able to puncture your thumbnail, such is their power. You can cut their heads off which not only solves the problem of those black 'nippers', but allows a good body scent of juices to leak into the water. I believe ragworm aren't as full of amino acids as a juicy lug, but doubtless they have some attraction when broken.

Common red ragworm grow to about seven inches and can be dug from estuaries where the mud is impregnated with coarse grit. They live in holes that are barely visible and pop their heads out only to secure some item of food with those pincers. They love firm mud so the actual digging is very messy and you'll get covered in muck. The most efficient way to dig them once you have located a good bed is by trenching (see Lugworm). They will also live in the cracks and crevices between red sandstone and soft limestone. They burrow deep into the layers of strata but can be broken out with a hammer and cold chisel. They live in a line usually below the low neap tides, so if you want to try cracking rocks open, make sure you do so as near the water's edge as possible, and dig on a low spring tide.

Ragworm are also good free swimmers, especially during the hours of darkness when they can be netted on the surface using a torch.

Ragworm

When I first heard of this technique quite honestly I didn't believe it. Having spent years digging them the hard way it seemed unlikely I could get the same worm simply by netting with a torch! However, on a sharking trip to Courtmacsherry in Ireland, I spent most nights on the pier in front of the Courtmacsherry Hotel trying for the conger eels that inhabit the stonework of the pier. One night I was standing with Mick Redding from Essex, when we both saw what looked like sandeels, snaking their way across the surface. Closer inspection with the torch revealed them to be big ragworm, swimming, and I assume feeding, freely. We didn't try netting them, but a shrimp net with an extendable handle would definitely have given us a few.

The other way to get good common ragworm is by contacting your local crabber. He will always have some because of the fact that ragworm live in the shells of hermit crabs (a good bait in their own right). Not every shell houses a bait of course, but enough do to be worth a try. Trawlers too, sometimes get the empty crab shells, which are old whelk shells as a by-product catch. You'll probably get a bucketful of shells if you ask nicely, and these can be cracked open with a hammer. Common red rag is a good bait for most species, but I would suggest it more as a summer bait than a winter one. They are excellent for all the flatfish family, plus whiting and small codling during the milder winter months.

If you are a mullet enthusiast, then sooner or later you will have to get round to collecting small red harbour rag. These come from very soft mud banks higher up the estuary and will be only an inch or two long. Whether they are a separate species, or just immature red rag I really couldn't say, but they make superb baits for mullet and smaller flatfish. You'll need a pair of waders to dig these little 'red men', and watch out for the very soft mud. Sometimes you can turn over twenty in a forkful of mud, but sort through the heap very carefully, and don't snatch or grab at them, otherwise they will break in two. When you have enough for a session, take them down to the tideline, rinse them clean in fresh seawater and dry them in folds of newspaper.

You can use a single harbour rag for a mullet bait, nicking the worm about halfway down its body, leaving the two ends wriggling freely. For flounders and dabs on the bottom, thread up to half a

Sea Fishing Baits

Look out something like an old seed tray, line it with paper and place your ragworm on top if you want to keep them for another session. Add some silver sand and they will stay active even longer, but winkle out those worms that die, otherwise they will kill off your whole tray.

dozen onto a small fine wire hook and cast out gently, they really are a delicate bait. Harbour rag can be dug in most muddy harbours and estuaries, but I am afraid they do not keep too well.

The best bait of the lot is called 'white gold' by beach match anglers, for the rarer white ragworm is a superlative small to medium fish bait. They can be dug from the same ground as the common red rag, but will also be found out on the open sandy/muddy beach when you are trench-digging lugworm. They are best used straight away, or if you have to keep them, put them in an aerated tank system as with lugworm. They will keep for several weeks, which is often just as well as they aren't too easy to come by. In fact I don't know of even one tackle dealer that supplies them to customers, although some professional diggers keep them by especially for a particular shop's match team.

They will keep in newspaper for a couple of days if kept cool, but they are better if treated like a livebait, for that is how they work best. Keep them in a separate plastic tank or bucket to the lugworm, and use the same plastic tubing to the aerator pump. If you are taking them to fish with, place them in a bucket of fresh seawater, but keep them well oxygenated, and use one of those battery-powered aerator

Ragworm

pumps available from most tackle shops. Maybe you didn't realise this, but if you are on a long haul drive to your favourite venue, you can make an adaption to run the aerator pump from your cigarette lighter in the car. It saves on batteries, which you then use only when fishing. Any worms you don't use can be transported back to your holding tank for another session.

King ragworms are the best bait in their category for very big bass, big cod, and big thornback. They are also the premier bait for stingray fishing, but the number of anglers fishing for stingrays is minimal on a nationwide basis. You can dig kings from amongst the common red rag, but they do have clearly defined areas. Sewer outfalls, and warm-water power station outfalls are good places to dig them. I remember fishing Hinkley Point power station once for big bass with Ken Flack, a local specialist, and as the tide dropped away, so Ken disappeared with a fork and came back an hour later, with the biggest kings I have ever seen. They weren't just long, they were as thick as your middle finger! These were used whole, and gave us a super bass of $8^{1}/_{4}$ lb. Most anglers who have located a ground for kings rarely disclose them, and I cannot blame them for that. Irresponsible digging will soon wipe out the stock, but an individual taking around a dozen will not dent the stocks too much.

I have never had any success in freezing down ragworm. They simply go mushy, and should be treated as a livebait. Wrapped in newspaper together with particle chips of moisture absorbing materials they can be kept for about a week if kept cool. You must, as with all worms, remove the dead ones immediately, otherwise they contaminate the remaining stock. All the ragworms can be kept for some period of time in an aerated tank in the garage, and they will tolerate a slightly warmer temperature than the lugworm. In Ireland, ragworm tend to just hang limply when held vertically, whereas those dug from the south coast of England will coil up on themselves, indicating a much stronger bait. Some anglers actually feed them in the tank, using tiny pieces of mussel, however I would advise using them as soon as possible, whenever weather and fishing conditions permit. After all, you don't catch fish with your bait in the tank!

In the north-east of England an enterprise is under way that

Sea Fishing Baits

consists of commercially rearing ragworm using 'aquaculture' techniques. Scientists have discovered that they can actually double the growth rate of farm-reared ragworm, over those that grow naturally in the wild. The two factors governing this are water temperature regulation and improved high nutrition food supply. At the moment the cost of running such an enterprise is high, somewhere around £250,000, but there is interest not only in England but in America as well. Using controlled conditions an egg will take only nine months to become a six-inch worm as opposed to two years under natural conditions. It is not dissimilar from the controlled environment in which Rainbow trout are reared, but as warm water was one of the major keys to success, they had to utilise some from a power station that normally allowed that pre-heated water to run straight into the sea. If you remember, Hinkley Point power station outfall gave us some colossal king rag. Output is hoped to grow to 25 million ragworm a year and should this prove a success the same controlled environment conditions may be used for peeler crabs. This is a step in the right direction to meet the growing demand on all aspects of our pressured environment. However, for me, bait digging by hand is still satisfying, if hard work, and I get particular pleasure from catching fish with a self-dug bait.

As a final pointer on obtaining ragworm I contacted one of my retired suppliers of quality worms, Brian Searle from Southsea. Brian has been a professional digger for around twenty years, working in the area from Chichester to Portsmouth. Some of his observations are certainly worth noting. For instance, he assures me that you can dig ragworm in anything from small loose shingle to estuary mud. The white rag which he referred to as 'snakes' will only come from clean white sand or ground shell beaches, whereas the common ragworm that he specialises in tolerates a much wider range of beach.

A common fallacy among anglers is that the colder it becomes, the deeper the worms go. This is not the case Brian assures me, as the temperature change in the sand or mud will vary little in relation to the air temperature. The best area for digging is about three quarters of the way down the tideline, the ragworm tending to stay in very defined areas. According to him, you can literally dig out an area of

Ragworm

You want King Ragworm? How about this two-foot-long specimen, that was cut into segments and used as flounder bait. The pincers on a ragworm this size demand a little respect!

worms through a fishing season, and next year not only will the stocks be replenished, but they will be in exactly the same area, not moving ten feet either way. His theory is that the worms stay in such a localised area due to some mineral substance in the beach that they require—perhaps like some animals need a salt block to lick. As for depth, that depends not on the air temperature, but on the quality of the ground you are digging. In loose shingle for instance, the ragworm can be up to two feet down, being able to burrow down easily. In hard white, almost china-clay-like ground, similar to that on the Isle of Wight where many good rag beds are, they may be only a foot down.

Brian's method of testing the ground is to jab the fork into the mud, and gently rock it back and forth to disturb the ragworm. If they are present, you should see tiny spurts of water from their holes and then you will know the area is worth digging. Another method is

Sea Fishing Baits

to stamp on the ground and watch for those same spurts of seawater. As an indication of what he feels a good rag bed should produce, in the last two hours of ebb and the first of flood, he would hope to produce about 500 to 1000 worms, all of which will have come from a clearly defined area.

The best way he thinks of storing them for a long time is in a bait tank. If you remove dead worms as soon as possible and put a freshly rinsed piece of seaweed in the tank, you can keep them for up to three months. Good aeration is important. This is around three times longer than I personally thought you could keep them. Temperature is the all important factor, and the best range to keep them in is around 45–48 degrees Fahrenheit. If it gets to 52 degrees you will start to lose them, the same goes if the temperature gets lower than around 38 °F. It is most important to keep a stable temperature, and this also goes for worms bought from your local tackle dealer.

Invariably shop worms will come with chips of vermiculite, which is a non-irritant roofing insulation with no glass fibre in it. This is added to remove any excess moisture, but Brian feels vermiculite is only good if you are going to use the bait immediately, as it tends to absorb a bit too much moisture and make the ragworm dehydrate, a factor which allows the body temperature to creep up, and the worms to die. The best way is to lay an entire newspaper in the bottom of an old seed tray, sprinkle on a layer of very fine silver sand, and lay the worms on this—it is important not to let them 'ball up' into a heap, but to spread them evenly. Treated like this they should keep for up to a week.

He believes the spawning period to run from around the end of November to March, at which time many worms will move to deeper water. When they return to recolonise those very same beds, it will be done at night, and many trawlermen have seen the sea alive with swimming ragworm when they have been hauling nets at night. You can tell when a ragworm is about to 'milk up' with eggs by turning it over and looking at its underside. If it is still a rusty red it will not spawn that season. But if it's green, it will spawn, becoming milky and too soft for use as a hookbait as it will fly off during the cast. He rarely digs if a particular bed he is working is full of spawning worms.

Ragworm

He says, quite rightly, that it is important to leave the spawners alone to ensure the next season's crop, and after twenty odd years in the bait-digging business it is a policy that ensures bait for the next generation of anglers.

Talking to Brian gave me the chance to get a pro-digger's idea about how much damage anglers can do to a ground. A pro-digger needs to get as much bait from a rag bed as he can, and in the shortest possible time. He doesn't waste fork time on a borderline bed, whereas the non-professional digger—the angler just out to get some bait for himself, can if he doesn't stop to think about the following season's stocks, decimate everything. Anglers have been known to dig up boat moorings, or dig too close to piers and generally cause problems that the pro-digger goes to great lengths to avoid. Anglers also tend to buy or dig too much bait, then waste the leftovers, which in turn puts undue pressure on the worm beds. Take only as much as you can fish a session with.

For all these reasons I prefer to buy my bait from a digger. I sometimes use a calculator to work out the quantity of bait I shall need. Admittedly I am usually working on a feature for a magazine or book, so I use three rods, and need a calculator! Into my calculation goes what species I am aiming for, how many hooks I have on each rod, how many hours of a certain state of tide I am going to fish, and how often I am going to wind in. I'll tell you now that I nearly always leave my baits out for half an hour, allowing enough time for the worm juices to drift around in the currents. If you get plenty of bites, or are fishing a tide run with weed then you adjust accordingly. Even so I can spend a six-hour session with three rods—two using three-hook paternosters, the other either a single or double-hook paternoster—and rarely get through 100 rag or lug worms. I beach fish alone most of the time, so three rods bother nobody.

These pointers from Brian Searle as a pro-digger should help you adjust your bait supply accordingly, and my latter tip might even catch you an extra fish or two. Don't keep winding in just so you can show everybody how far you can cast! Catching fish is really what it's all about!

Squid

If you don't like things that squirm, stick to you and squirt a rich black ink then read no further. But of course, if you don't, you would be missing out on some very good sea baits, so I'll continue! It might seem a trifle strange but squid and octopus are molluscs; it is just that their shell is almost non-existent. Their arms are extremely mobile and are used for shooting out from the coiled position to grab any prey that comes too close to them. They have a sort of parrot-beak jaw which extends from the mouth to take any food the arms bring to it. The arms are equipped with many suckers which line the undersides and these have amazing sticking power.

There are two types of squid I feel are important to the angler. The best is the small baby 'calamari' squid which is around six inches in length and available from fishmongers in boxes, ideal for freezing down. Alternatively you can buy them already frozen, in large boxes, break them down into smaller blocks using a mallet or hammer, and use them for cod in the winter, and conger in the summer.

Both the cod and conger will take one of these calamari squid whole, but for cod I like to mount them on a double-hook rig. That way you can strike earlier and still have an excellent chance of a strong hookhold. The conger are less fussy, and you can mount one whole on a larger hook leaving your striking time later. For small fish, and black or red bream spring to mind, you can cut up the squid into long thin strips which when hooked once or twice will wave enticingly in the tidal current. The squid's flesh should be pure white and will be very, very tough enabling you to use it more than once if you unhook carefully. The disadvantage is that squid, while it freezes well, tends to go 'off' quickly in hot weather. All it does is to soften a little, but the smell more than anything will tell you it's time to throw your leftovers over the side!

The other type of squid is just a large whole specimen of maybe two or three pounds in weight. Obviously far too large to be used as a hookbait on its own, you must clean it with a knife and rinse the dissected flesh in clean sea water. On no account use fresh water as this only makes the squid go 'off' quicker. These squid can also be purchased from the fish shop. Some tackle dealers keep a freezer in their shop and may also have some frozen squid for sale. I hesitate to

This is the sort of huge catch made by the author, Norman Message and Bob Edwards on the boat '4 Pints'. Several of these cod top 20lb.

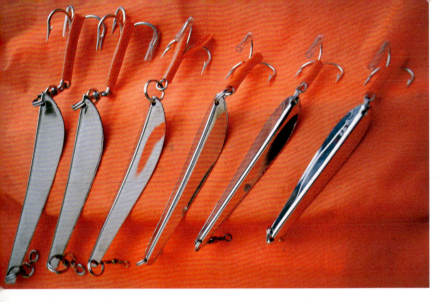

Ryobi market some of the best shop bought pirks in a wide variety of different sizes to suit varying depths and tidal conditions.

Facing page: First to realise the significance of the longer slim-style chromed pirks were the small boat dinghy anglers from Tony's Tackle Shop in Eastbourne. They made huge catches of cod and pollock on this shaped pirk which was first used by top angler Norman Message on his boat '4 Pints'.

Artificial rubber sandeels are now so well made that their action in the water makes them a first class lure after live sandeel.

The use of the redgill rubber sandeel revolutionised pollock fishing—that huge cavernous mouth being just the right shape to fold up an eel and swallow.

This Ryobi range of Odin lures are excellent for bass, coalfish, pollock and mackerel from the shore. They come in different colours and weights. It may be better to change the wire treble hook to a heavier version if you have to swing your fish up cliffs.

Left: These are the curved hookshanks with a tube of rubber pulled over the top. They work best over deep water, and where the fish are very thick, in large shoals. They have been outdated by the better action redgill sandeel.

Facing page: Catch of pollock taken by the author using artificial sandeel aboard the 'Jan Steen' skippered by Bear Havinga, from Crookhaven in Ireland.

These small spinners from the Ryobi stable are very good for mackerel spinning from either shore or boat. The version with the single hook can be rigged the same as mackerel feathers.

Above: Additives are definitely here to stay. The author took these shore cod using a different additive on each bait. The result of course proves nothing, only that fish weren't put off by them!

Facing page: Thornback skate like this super seven pounder landed by a Welsh angler have a liking for an additive of pilchard oil and sodium laurel sulphate, or liquid emulsifier. The latter keeps the oil down near the sea bed where the fish can find it.

Overleaf: Nigel Newport of Western Fuels is after conger eel, and simply lowers his bait down the side of the pier for the predators that lurk beneath.

Squid

See what I mean about small fish working on big fish? This shore cod was landed by the author on lug and squid cocktail, then coughed up this whiting, which perhaps was nibbling around the same bait. It often pays off when big cod are around from the shore to leave a hooked whiting, pouting or poor cod, out for an extra half hour.

say catch your own, as buying in the shop is far more dependable, but in the warmer waters of the tropics they can be taken using a special squid jig, which consists of a conical lead with surface-mounted clusters of spikes. Dropped down at great depths they are jigged up towards the surface. Any squid attempting to entangle the lure, which it presumably mistakes for a fish, gets 'stabbed' by one of the spikes, and is hauled to the surface. You can do a similar trick in our waters, by rigging a series of three or four treble hooks in tandem, weighting and baiting the bottom one, with a strip of fish. When the squid attacks the fluttering bait its tentacles get tangled on the trebles.

Squid are incredibly fast swimmers. Working on the principle of jet propulsion, they go from static to 'where-did-that-go?' in a flash, usually when alarmed.

Sea Fishing Baits

I once had the privilege of seeing live squid feed on the edge of the coral barrier reef in Mauritius, on the Indian Ocean. They finned their way through the surface layers, stalking small fish and grabbing them in those sucker-ridden tentacles. There is a species of monster squid reputed to live in the black depths of the Humboldt current, a cool water artery in the Pacific Ocean. It is feared by local natives who refuse to venture out after dark, and who could blame them when estimates of these monsters range up to 35 feet in length and 500 lb in weight.

All squid carry a bag of ink which they squirt at enemies when threatened and I saw one do this only recently. We were bottom fishing off Hook Head in County Wexford on Ireland's south coast. I had a home-made set of flasher feathers and was deep jigging for whiting near the bottom. I had already had what I thought were fish striking at the feathers, but had failed to hook up. Eventually I dragged a most unusual fighting fish to the surface. Every time I dropped the rod to pump, it would pull hard downwards. Then I saw the culprit. A two-foot-long squid that had grabbed at the flashers and hooked itself on one tentacle! Jets of water and ink squirted a couple of feet in the air as it struggled and I watched with admiration the speed and force it attained with its jet propulsion; it obviously gave it some turn of speed. What we should have done with a beautiful fresh specimen like that was to eat it, but we were anglers, and after putting it in a bucket to watch its colours change, we began cutting it up for bait. As stated previously, the smaller calamari squid can be used whole as a hookbait, but bigger squid such as the one we had caught, need to be 'stripped'.

To do this, first you wash it thoroughly in a bucket of seawater to make sure all that ink is out. Then you peel and scrape off the outer skin, which should come off like wet cling film. This will leave the white flesh showing, but you need to slit along the edge to take out the guts, ink bag and backbone, which is akin to a piece of plastic. If you get ink on the skinned white flesh it will be difficult to get off. The head and tentacles are simply pulled away; the tentacles being used for smaller strip baits, while the head is used whole for big cod or conger. Once the body is opened out flat you can strip it into

Squid

A small calamari squid mounted whole is devastating for big cod. You won't get a bite every few seconds, but you can be sure it will be a good fish that picks it up and swims off with it.

whatever size segments the species and hook size demands.

I doubt you will have much success catching your own, but if you do snag some fresh squid, use them immediately, they are superb baits. If you go to the trouble of contacting local crabbers or netters you may stand a chance of getting two or three recently-caught squid from them. Use one for bait, and freeze the others down.

A convenient and comparatively clean bait to use, squid must be one of the top two boat-fishing baits.

Octopus

The octopus is not as rare as you would think, for we get quite a few round the British coastline, and some areas even have populations of their own. They are adapted more for crawling than swimming, and tend to pounce on their prey as it ventures near their rock caverns. While the squid is a creature of the open oceans, the octopus is a bottom dweller that sneaks up on fish and crabs. Reputed to be intelligent, they are masters of the art of camouflage, and blend in with their surroundings. I have only caught small octopuses when bottom fishing with baits in the U.K. and they ended up being 'stripped' down and sent to the bottom for other more worthy specimens. If you have never tried eating them then do so. I personally prefer calamari squid, which has a rubbery texture, but others enjoy octopus which has more flavour even though the tentacles are tougher.

The octopus has a strange breeding cycle, which is different for each species. The female common octopus however lays a few hundred eggs in a rock pile which she guards fervently for three weeks, during which time she will kill any other octopus that ventures near. After they hatch though she dies in a few days. The octopus has eight arms and only one row of suckers on each arm for the species that frequent our coast—the common octopus has two rows of suckers on each arm and is confined to our channel coastline. Fresh octopus is always difficult to come by, chiefly because it is sought by the restaurants, but frozen, they are available from supermarkets, although they are expensive. If you can resist the urge to eat one, cut it up and put it on the hook. If you gut it down and strip it up like a squid, it will freeze very well and make a tough bait.

Cuttlefish

I guess we have all seen budgies gnawing away on their cuttlefish, but the last place you expect it to come from is the sea. However it is a superb bait, maybe even better than squid. The common cuttlefish is about twelve inches long and ventures into shallow water to spawn over sand. They have a back colour of muted black and white but still have the tentacles and inky defence mechanism of the squid. It is their backbone that is the dried white material that you see either washed up on the beach, or displayed in pet shops for Joey the budgie. There is another smaller species of about five inches in length, but that is confined to Scottish waters. The common cuttlefish also has two longer 'grabbing' tentacles which it shoots out to hold prey on pads covered with those suction discs. They freeze extremely well, but make sure when you use them that the ink is well washed out, the skin removed, and the bait cut into strips. Then when you go fishing you just bait up your hook and drop it down.

Every single species of fish you can think of will take a piece of cuttlefish, the only thing that determines the species is the size of bait you use. Only recently I was out in a small, high-powered boat, fishing a mark off the Sussex coast. Norman Message runs his 17-foot Pilot the '4 Pints' way offshore to fish the wrecks in deep water, primarily with long slim pirks. On this occasion he had located a new rough ground mark where huge cod and sizeable conger would take nothing else but cuttlefish. I found it hard to believe, but after several fish had fallen to Norman's rod, I had to change my mackerel. The conger and cod hammered the cuttlefish almost as soon as it touched bottom.

I'm not aware of any particular smell to cuttlefish, but am prepared to believe it gives off some unknown smell, much like the amino acids in lugworm, because the fish love it. I finished the day with many fish, including three cod over 20 lb (the largest 23 lb) and all on a hot July day. Another possible reason for this success is that whereas squid feeds on other live fish, the cuttlefish has a preferred diet of crabs, prawns and shrimps. For this reason it must live on or near the bottom . . . and the fish that feed there come into contact with more cuttle than they do squid, which swim much higher. Either theory is acceptable, just get your hands on some cuttlefish!

Crabs

Crabs are possibly—no, definitely—the best shore bait you can ever use. I have no hesitation in saying this as it is not just my humble opinion, but that of hundreds of anglers across the nation. Whether it's because crabs are the main diet for inshore bottom-dwelling fish I don't know, but certainly for quality fish they are deadly. I have seen peeler crab consistently outfish any other bait so many times it doesn't bear thinking about. They are easily collected although I must confess that collecting crabs is not my favourite pastime, especially when it involves lifting half a ton of rock and stuffing my arm underneath in the dark. It's not a case of being wimpish, it's just that a big edible crab grabbing a stray finger has the capability to crack a bone with ease. Let a tiny crab nip you and you begin to realise a little common-sense should really prevail.

Most anglers feel that the best crab is the peeler, which is merely the species of any crab that is in the process of casting its old shell. The hard fact is that a peeler spends most of its time hiding under a rock when in this stage, so fish are rarely likely to come across them anyway. What fish will find are the ordinary green hardbacks, so why not use hardbacks as a bait? If we try to look at crabs logically it is the angler that is more interested in peelers than the fish themselves although I accept that there may be some body secretions from a peeler crab as it changes shells that could make the peeler special. However, if you examine the stomach contents of fish like cod, conger and bass, you will find only hardback crabs inside, either small edibles or green shore crabs.

Let's take an in-depth look at the crab so you understand a bit more about them. The shell on the outside of the crab is really the skeleton, which doesn't live, and is the only means of protection for the vulnerable insides of the crab. In order to grow, the crab needs to shuck off this outer skeleton and grow a new one. It's at this stage that it becomes a peeler crab and is the one the angler should spend time collecting. The crabs draw in calcium from the old shell, and it is this which makes the top shell very brittle and hard. To remove the shell, the crab starts to draw in sea water and uses it to expand and push the old shell off. It does this in maybe half a day, starting to form a new shell immediately, and hardening it by making use of that

Crabs

calcium it drew from the old shell. The peeler is the stage at which the angler wants to use them, but when they start to firm up on the new shell they are called crispies, leatherbacks or softbacks.

They all make good baits, but remember that shell is hardening all the time, so if you have them stored in a tank, or plastic container with an aeration system, you may come to use them and find the shell harder than you thought. Under natural conditions this hardening will take about a week, but this process is also dependent on water and air temperature. As with the worms previously described, the lower the temperature you can keep them in, the longer they will stay comatose, and therefore softer.

As it is temperature that governs this shell change, you could do worse than start your collecting near the top of the tide line as this area will receive the warmth of the sun for a longer period. That way, you are able to work down the tide as it drops, hopefully gaining more time to collect the softies or peelers. The female breeds only when she is soft, so anytime you see a pair or crabs locked together you can be fairly sure the one underneath is a female and therefore, a bait. Females with eggs usually move off to deeper water, where it is thought they search for a higher salinity level in the water.

The best way to test if a crab is a peeler is to twist the last segment of the rear leg. As crabs can regenerate limbs, it is a useful way to check for soft baits. If the removed segment reveals nothing or a firm white muscle then the crab is a hardback. Leave it where you found it unless you are purposely using hardbacks. If though, the leg is of soft new meat, you have yourself a peeler. While hardbacks have a uniform colour, the peeler may be blotchy or even mottled.

If you turn over kelp-covered boulders or rocks in the quest for crabs, be sure to watch out for any broken glass. For this reason it's best to use an old pair of gardening gloves, and wash them out in fresh water after use to prevent the salt rotting the material. It's also a good way to avoid getting a severe nip from a big edible.

Experienced crab collectors can tell just by looking at the crab whether it's a peeler or not, but give it a gentle squeeze when you pick it up, and it should have a slightly soapy touch, with bubbles at the edge. These occur because the crab has increased its body size by

Sea Fishing Baits

filling with water; you can peel off the old shell. I must confess as a youngster I spent several seasons fishing with peeler crab on the hook, and not being very impressed with them. How come everybody else caught fish? Why was it presented in the magazines as being the best bass bait etc? Then someone took me quietly aside and showed me that you had to peel off the shell and legs to reveal the soft crab underneath! Well, I always was a slow learner!

If you have a large edible don't forget that they too can peel, and while far too large for a single hookbait, they can be cut down to make several baits. Want to know what's a helluva good bait for big shore conger? Try mounting a whole, peeled edible crab on a big single hook and you have about the best shore conger bait there is.

Even if your stretch of coastline isn't what we call 'graunchy' or rough ground, you can still set up your own crab-collecting operation. In the north-east of England many beach match anglers put out old tyres on the low water open beaches where crabs can be found. These spots are then checked at each low tide, sometimes in the middle of the night, to see when the crabs are in the peeler stage. I don't recommend you start littering the local holiday beach with a stack of old tyres, just that it's sometimes possible to do this on the more remote beaches. Match fishing being the competitive sport it is, however, means that there are those people about who will think nothing of stealing from the tyres laid down by their fellow anglers, but should it occur to you to try this, take care—it isn't unknown for these anglers to put broken glass in the tyres to deter people from stealing their bait.

Another method of collecting crabs if you live near a creek with muddy banks, is to push old bean cans, or similar, into the mud, about three quarters of the way down the bank. The crabs will soon take up residence, although the tins may eventually rust away in the saltwater.

The best way to store what you have collected is by following the advice given on all the other baits—i.e. keep them cool. To do this, put them in a clean plastic bucket, and cover them with damp seaweed. If you need to keep hardbacks that's no problem as they should stay live for up to five or six days providing you top up with

Crabs

A bucketful of peeler crabs ready to use. Don't waste the small legs and claws, they all combine to make up a bait or two when you run out of crab bodies.

fresh seaweed. The peelers and softies are more delicate and for anything longer than a two-day session, you'll have to go to the expense of keeping them in an old fridge in the garage. Of course if you already are rigged up for storing ragworm and lugworm as previously described you save a lot of time and trouble. The crabs should be ready to peel if possible, stored at either side of 40 °F, and kept moist.

Crabs breathe through their gills, and the breathing action can be seen when tiny bubbles are blown out from their gills. If you make the mistake of completely covering them with seawater the entire process of peeling and re-shelling will start, and the last thing you want is a bucketful of hardbacks, especially when you have gone to so much trouble to get peelers! If any crabs die, remove them immediately

Sea Fishing Baits

otherwise they will contaminate the remaining stock. Keep changing the seaweed every day if possible, or at least every third day, otherwise the crabs will start to die. I have known them kept for nearly a month like this, but usually you will have already used them to catch some fish, and should have topped up the stock anyway. If you use a square or rectangular plastic container, you can quarter it by slotting in hardboard or plywood partitions. That way you can segregate peelers from softies, and the occasional hardbacks, plus you can then rotate your holding stock and not mix fresh specimens with old. Use them as soon as fishing conditions allow, and you will make the most of a fresh bait.

Crabs can peel all year round, depending on the temperature, but are more prolific in the late spring and mid autumn. This also coincides with the best of the bass fishing. Specialists after this species say the bass actually move in because that's the time they know most peeler activity is taking place, but as I said previously, most crabs in the peeler stage know they are vulnerable and will therefore be hiding out of any predator's way. I feel the bass may in fact move in to feed on whitebait which is also at a naturally prolific high level in those months.

As for the actual baiting up of crabs, there is only one method that is good for me, and that puts fish on the beach. You need to make a proper crab hook since despite my investigations with Partridge hooks, there is not a specific crab hook available for anglers. You can make your own from paper clip wire and an ordinary bass hook. A crab bait is by nature generally bulky, so you need a hook with a wide gape, otherwise your hook might bury itself in the bait rather than the fish you seek. Also peeler is a delicate bait, and needs to be tied to the hook using elasticated cotton. The resultant bait will be bound down for casting so it looks like an unsavoury blob, but I assure you it will still catch fish.

The first thing you do with a crab is to peel off the top shell followed by the plates from the underside. Pull off the legs and claws but keep them aside, as when you run out of bodies, you can peel and use the legs and claws. Waste nothing. If it is a large peeler you need to cut it in half and bind both halves separately to the hook with the

Crabs

elastic cotton. Although there's no need to knot the cotton as it binds down into the meat when you pull it tight, personally I tie mine off with a half hitch. It gets a bit fiddly when you want to rebait as you have to snap off the knotted thread, but I don't mind too much, as at least I know the bait has been secured well and is not likely to fly off the hook. Peelers aren't too agressive, but the hardbacks will be out to nail you, so press on the top of their shell to immobilise them, and always handle from behind. I see no point in letting them nip you! The hardbacks need no cotton to tie them to the hook, but they should not be used for distance casting. Especially in the use of peelers or softies, as well as tying them down, you should clip your bait down using one of the many up or down methods of supporting baits for the cast.

Hardbacks generally explode in a million fragments on the power cast, and are far better suited to wrasse fishing from the rocks, where all that is required is a gentle lob of thirty yards, or a drop vertically down a rock face into deep water. Wrasse devour the small hardbacks avidly, and have no trouble crunching them up with those molars. Rather than leger them hard on the bottom it's best to suspend them a couple of feet off the seabed by means of a paternoster. That way you are isolating the crab in a position where the wrasse can easily spot it. If you leger them hard on the bottom, a hardback crab will scuttle off into the nearest snag as sanctuary, in which case you end up losing your gear!

The only other crab that can be collected is the hermit crab. These really are excellent baits, especially for cod, and can usually be procured from trawlers or crabbers who get them as a by-product catch. Of course they are no use to the commercial fishermen, but you might come to some sort of agreement whereby he keeps them for you. The hermit crab lives in empty whelk shells, which it utilises as a sort of mobile home, carrying it on his back wherever he goes. It is also a form of protection against predators, as the hermit has a very soft carapace or shell, and is almost the same as a peeler. Occasionally you may have the good fortune to find a ragworm living in the extreme spiral end of the shell, and then you get two baits at once!

Sea Fishing Baits

The best way to get a hermit crab out of its shell is by breaking the shell with a hammer, but don't take a big swing at it, otherwise all you will end up with is hermit pâté. Tap away until the shell breaks up and then you can get at the bait inside. Hermits are best kept in damp seaweed in their shell homes until ready for use, and don't leave them too long, they aren't the best of keepers. Damp seaweed changed each day, may give you a four-day optimum period of usage at the best.

Finally don't neglect regular edible crabs. Sometimes crabbers have an excess of edibles that may have died overnight in their holding cages and are therefore unsaleable in the market. Do not let these go to waste, as the meat inside, although possibly doubtful for human consumption, is of the highest quality for hookbaits. After breaking open the claws, legs and shell, the meat inside can be levered or cut out, and whipped on to the hook using elasticated thread. It should catch any of the species that a peeler will, and is a favourite bait for big bass and conger. In high summer it is also a favourite with the other crabs in the water which can strip it in a few minutes. If you don't get a bite in about twenty minutes, wind in and see how much is left.

Mullet anglers, fishing where the crab and lobster boats berth, make full use of this edible, as crushed and dropped in for groundbait, it is one of the best mullet attractants. A tiny piece of crab claw meat on a size 10 freshwater hook, floatfished in the centre of this groundbait will give you a better than even shot at hooking a good mullet. I have even caught pollock, wrasse, mackerel and mullet on left overs of cooked lobster, but it's such a tasty dish, there very often isn't much in the way of leftovers!

Artificials

The modern bait fisherman must be aware of the current availability of artificial lures that can be used to catch sea fish. While there have been innovations like scented plastic worms, oiled plastic crabs and the like, they have never been any real threat to fresh live worms, or a juicy fish strip of meat with the blood still oozing out.

While it must be appreciated that all fish use their olfactory or 'smell' organs as the primary location factor, there comes a time when they visually feed. Usually this occurs only in clear water, but I have a feeling that vibration is an even more important factor in aiding their location of a lure.

Many species feed at night, and I have always believed that a strong smelling bait would be the best bet to bring your target species in, but recently I have had a change of thought.

The top wrecking boat out of Newhaven in Sussex visits the homes of conger, ling and big cod regularly, often returning with many thousands of pounds of fish. Usually they fish all day, but on a couple of sessions when they stayed until after dark, they were amazed to discover that the cod were still hammering their lures in pitch dark! Even in full daylight in deep water the light penetration must be almost zero, yet fish are still caught, so they must surely use that lateral line full of nerves to locate the lure! It's worth thinking about, because the modern angler's armoury should always call for at least some lures, both from boat and shore.

For the boat angler, possibly the most popular fish-catching artificial lure is called a pirk. This can either be bought or you can make one yourself. A pirk is either a straight metal bar from three inches to ten inches in length, or a length of lead-filled chrome tubing. To get down quickly to the fish and remain on the seabed a pirk will weigh anything from 6 oz to $1^{1}/_{2}$ lb, and consequently they can become expensive when you consider you might get through six at a session—particularly if you're fishing a snaggy piece of rough ground, or around the superstructure of a wreck.

There are several shop-bought models to choose from, and quite frankly they are all pretty good. One brand stands out as the best though, and this is the range of Norwegian Solvkroken Jiggers.

They are available in four different sizes, 6 oz (175 gm), 9 oz

Sea Fishing Baits

(250 gm), 14 oz (400 gm) and 17½ oz (500 gm). These are made from polished, heavy gauge stainless-steel metal, designed to withstand some pretty heavy punishment. They are vertically triangular, and flutter well when dropped down to the seabed. A large treble, with the shank covered in red plastic tubing completes the lure, and it remains one of the most highly effective for deep-water jigging. These four sizes are the best for extreme depths, but the whole range in fact runs right back down to 1 oz. These lighter-sized Solvkrokens are best for shallower water, say over thirty feet, but up to 100 feet.

The Abu tackle company also market a range of pirks for the fishermen. They range from 28 gm to almost half a kilo in several different patterns. I would use them more for medium tackle reef fishing, with the Egon being downright deadly for shore casting for mackerel in the lighter sizes. The Egon can be worked quite slowly as all of the weight is in the lower half of the pirk. Weights are available in 28, 60, 100, 150 and 200 gm.

Then there is the Lucas pirk. This sinks quickly and wobbles from side to side. The range offers the following weights: 28, 40, 60, 100, 150, 200 and 300 gm. The Prisma is an old model but still works very well for cod, pollock and even big whiting. It offers a big area of reflection, has a wide-angled swing movement and is available in the 100 and 200-gm weights. The Sextett is probably based on the original-shaped pirk that proved popular with British boat fishermen during the cod boom of the late 1960s. The Sextett comes in three weights: 100, 200 and 400 gm. The Klaus and Borge pirks are scaled and sink quickly.

The best of the range in my opinion is the new Rondo slim pirk which comes in 100, 150, and 200-gm weights, and confirms what I have found from my own experiences: the heavy, wide-angle flutter of many pirks are great for attracting fish, but the action is so violent that they often miss the lure on the strike, or get foulhooked. The Rondo slim, or indeed any long, slim pirk is often grabbed crosswise by, shall we say, a cod. On the upward sweep of the strike the slim pirk will slide through their jaws and bang up against the corner of the jaw, making for a good hookhold.

Artificials

This was first shown to me by Norman Message on the boat '4 Pints' out of Eastbourne, Sussex. Norman does a lot of long-distance wrecking trips and has a tremendous catch record. He makes his pirks out of long chrome tubing, about eight inches long by half an inch wide, and fills the lower half with lead. Another home-made pirk is made by him from a simple piece of chromed hexagonal steel bar, with an angle cut each end. In small sizes of three or four inches with a large treble, this hexagonal pirk is a killer for bass.

A pirk is used basically to imitate a live fish swimming near the bottom, but fishing one properly is not an easy task. A long rod is essential, as the lure is allowed to hit the seabed and then, with the reel in gear, it is swept upwards using the tip of the rod. A strike can come at any period during the rise and fall of the pirk.

A pirk with some mackerel or squid draped over each hook point is also excellent for deep-water ling. I have no idea why, but a baited pirk will often catch more ling than just a bait fished on the bottom.

The pirk is a fairly basic instrument, with a split ring and large treble at one end, and a split ring for attaching your mainline at the other. Many of the shop-bought models come with very strong hooks. Bearing in mind that you are bouncing that lure up and down in the lower four feet of water, the chances of snagging are high; with a strong treble you will lose every pirk you snag. What many anglers are doing now is to change the heavy-duty treble for a larger, thinner-gauge wire one. When you hook a fish you take it nice and steady and you shouldn't lose him. But if you snag in the bottom, you can lock the reel drag up, point the rod top at the line and steam the boat away, letting the finer wire points spring out under the pressure. They can then be bent back into shape using a pair of pliers.

As well as putting some strips of bait on the trebles for attractants, you can put some of those plastic squids over them. First you take the treble off the split ring, cut the tip off the squid head and slide it down over the treble eye. Then attach it to the split ring again. There is one fluorescent pale green squid that glows in the dark, and I have had success with this. Also you can add some flash to your old pirks by wrapping them in silver or coloured tape. Norman Message had a short stubby pirk with yellow tape bands around it, which he swore

Sea Fishing Baits

was the best he had ever used. I know whenever I fished with him, his catch rate exceeded those of the rest of us put together!

Making pirks at home is cheap and enjoyable, because you can make the colours as complex as your heart desires. And one of the best colours? I'm afraid it's black, which rather proves my original theory that fish home in on them more because of their vibration rather than any visual merit.

While pirks are popular with bottom fish, they will also be avidly devoured by midwater species like pollock and coalfish. One method if you don't get a hit on the drop down, and after a few seconds jigging, is to point your rod down the line and wind like crazy. It's called 'speedwinding' and coalfish especially will crash one of these fast-moving lures. A far more efficient way to fish for these two species is by using an artificial sandeel lure. You have already heard how effective live sandeel can be, and I still say there is nothing to beat a fresh livebait. However, many anglers will be unable to get hold of live eels just to suit their trip out and will have to use one of two lures.

The Norwegian Solvkroken company offer imitation rubber eels on a fairly basic terminal rig that consists of a hook with a bend in the shank, and a swivel at the other end. Over this you slide a coloured piece of plastic tubing. When retrieved the bend in the hook shank makes the lure twist and wobble, supposedly imitating a wounded sandeel. When small fish are thick on the ground pollock and coalfish will beat their way past these to grab the lures but they are not too successful for catching larger fish.

For the 'biggies' you need to use the largest size redgill artificial rubber sandeel, which is devastatingly effective, and has a built-in tail wiggle that is pure seduction for pollock and coalfish. I would even go so far as to say, that since the introduction of this sandeel lure on the market, pollock fishing as we previously knew it, has been revolutionised. Most anglers will have a few redgills in their tackle box, and if they haven't, they should do.

These lures are best fished from a drifting boat, with a light breeze to push the craft along, and a strong tide to make the predators active. You need to rig with a long flowing trace, as the eel must

Artificials

obviously look as lifelike as possible. If you put the lead too near the eel it will kill that tail-wiggling action, which is what makes it so successful. It's also important to fish with a lead lighter than you would normally use to touch bottom. If the line is going straight down then the retrieve will mean the eel is swimming vertically, which in its natural state, it rarely, if ever, does, The lighter lead will allow the line to come back to you at an inclined angle, and the takes will be more confident. It's also possible to use the redgill at anchor, something which not many anglers realise. At anchor, providing you have a fair run of tide, you can make that eel work by using a very light lead, sometimes as small as one or two ounces.

The pollock and coalfish will be feeding into a tide current if it is running hard, searching for the shoals of sandeel that will also be swimming into the current. A tip here might help you, something I found out myself, by accident. When the tide runs hard most baitfish swim, or rather battle, against the current low to the bottom where the flow is slowed somewhat by the friction with the seabed. The pollock will also be working deeper, so when you drop, then retrieve your lure during the strongest tidal flow, do not come up too far. If you are judging the distance by counting the number of times you turn the reel handle, make it, say twenty turns. When the tide eases, those same baitfish will rise off the bottom followed by the pollock and coalfish, swimming through a greater variance of depths. Therefore you must bring your lure higher in the water to maximise your chances of a take—say forty turns of the reel handle. Also if slack water coincides with sunset the fish will naturally rise much higher towards the surface, so therefore bring your lure up to maybe sixty or seventy turns. It's only a small point, but it's one of those bits of knowledge that makes a fair angler a good one.

While the Solvkroken rubber tubing eels are perfectly good to use for shore casting for bass, pollock and coalfish, the smaller version of those same redgills will outfish them every time. Again you will have to use a long tail from lead to eel, in order for it to retain the most lifelike appearance. This length will be limited by the length of your rod, but as a general guide I would say don't drop it below five feet if you have a heavy lead of two ounces.

Sea Fishing Baits

In both shore and boat use of this artificial sandeel, it is of paramount importance not to strike at any bite. What happens when a pollock or coalfish takes is this. In its natural state the eel is quite long, anything from seven inches to twelve inches if it's a launce. The pollock takes the eel from behind by opening its mouth quickly and sucking the eel back. As it does so it folds the eel into its mouth for swallowing, and therefore any premature striking at the initial plucks where the pollock is sucking at the bait, merely means a missed fish. What you must do is to just keep winding the reel until the fish has sucked in the eel, folded it over for swallowing, and closed its mouth. If you follow this rule you will nail every fish that hits.

The redgill sandeel is a must in the tackle box, and in the right hands will catch far more pollock and coalfish than an angler using bait.

Muppets

This strange-sounding name applies to the range of plastic squid marketed by many companies—in Britain, primarily by the Shakespeare company. They have been around for a few years now and are an artificial bait that every angler should have. Muppets are also known as Wondershine squid; they were popularised on the east coast by the northern anglers who added them uptrace of their conventional pirks to catch cod. They come in many different sizes, and although representing no particular natural baitfish, they certainly do work. Primary species when fishing a set of four on either a lead or pirk would be cod, pollock and coalfish. However you can buy the larger sized squids individually and use them as described in the pirk chapter, for draping over the shank of a pirk's treble hook. Another point worth noting is that the light green coloured muppet will glow in the dark, and I have even used them singly to slide over the top of any fish bait I have been using when bottom fishing. It may be my imagination, but I have now had enough weird takers on them that I wouldn't class as visual feeders—thornbacks, conger and even bull huss—to take them seriously.

Artificials

If you fish a running leger rig over rough ground, and like to fish a small hook as a flyer about three feet off the bottom, then try sliding the light green squid over the flyer bait. It draws big bream and pouting like a magnet! I have used American-made squids for years in foreign climes, but they are used primarily to imitate the natural baby squid in flight from a predator, and are trolled across the surface, skipping through the waves. Larger plastic squid of up to 15 inches are trolled in similar fashion for Bluefin tuna over 1,000 lb in weight, but why they work so well in British waters, and on bottom gear, is beyond me.

The Shakespeare series of squids, or 'muppets' as they are affectionately known, come four to a trace, each mounted on a 3/0 hook. They come in red, green or pink. The larger packs of six come unmounted and not on hooks so you can make up whatever size trace you want. Individual colours are pink, blue, white, red, green and black. My advice is to stick to just three: pink, green and black. Some of the best for deep jigging for cod are the multi-coloured Wondershine squid which come as three-feathered hooks. Your best bet would be to buy a load of individual colours, make them up into trace lengths, or paternoster rigs to suit your own fishing, and try to add one of those Cyalume chemical lights in green to fix either inside the squid skirt or just above the hook. For deep dropping on pollock and cod, a set of these Cyalumes fished in conjunction with a chromed pirk for weight can be absolutely deadly! A small tip, and never written about in the UK press before—so now you know how I catch my fish!

Feathers and Spoons

Feathers, when whipped to a hook shank in several fibres and wetted down, can look like a tiny eel or whitebait. This is undoubtedly what many species take them for, and why they are so successful. You can either buy sets of feathers from the tackle shop, or make up your own. They aren't exactly expensive, but I personally get more satisfaction from catching fish on feathers I have made up myself

Sea Fishing Baits

than from buying a set. They are one of the oldest artificial lures, and it is only comparatively recently that any design advances have been made.

Basically they are a set of four or six hooks fixed to the line paternoster style, with a lead or pirk at the bottom, and a swivel at the top for attaching to the reel line. Hen feathers were a favourite choice being cheap to obtain. They were dyed a variety of colours (which we now know probably wouldn't have had too much bearing on catches). A big hunk of feathers on a big hook were called cod feathers, while the smaller strands whipped to the smaller hookshank were called mackerel feathers. Unfortunately I have had cod on mackerel feathers and vice-versa so it doesn't seem to make too much difference as far as individual species goes.

Most fish will have been taken on feathers at some time or other, but recently I have had resounding success with what I call 'flashers'. I first used these in the Isles of Scilly where I soon noticed more species were being caught on these than feathers. I made them up from unravelled Mylar piping which was recently popular in dressing trout flies, and then started making sets up, by sliding a piece of silicon tubing one inch long over the hook, up over the eye and onto the snood line. I then stuck some silver sellotape either side of the hookshank so it stuck, put a twist in it near the hook eye, and rolled the silicon tubing back over the hook eye and covering the end of the tape. I even went to the trouble of cutting a little V-shaped tail in it, and I can tell you I hammer a wide variety of species on them. I never use feathers now, they are outdated by the modern silver, copper or gold materials available which simply do a better job.

While on the subject of things that flash, the same principle of using anything that catches the light and throws it towards a fish, can be applied to bottom fishing. For years anglers caught flounders and plaice using a ragworm that trundled along the seabed behind a flashing white plastic, or silver metal spoon. It was so effective it could outfish a standard worm anytime. That was used from a drifting boat, either in an estuary or over a sandbank. Occasionally anglers would use it when rowing along slowly during periods of slack high water, or when there was no wind to drift the boat. It was

Artificials

but a short step when anglers heard of big cod being caught with plastic cups jammed in their throats (these cups would have been discarded by passenger vessels, and sunk to the bottom where the cod engulfed them) to the realisation that since there is little or no smell to a plastic cup, the cod must have been attracted to them because of their light colour. Could not the flashing flounder spoon work for cod?

It was first tried I believe off the Needles in winter, where catches were deemed to be better than those gained using static baits. There is such a strong tidal flow in this area that the blade could be made to flash, even when fishing at anchor. I remember well taking some thornbacks using my own version of a flashing spoon, and recall how excited I was. From here anglers developed end traces that took up to four flashing spoons in a row, and still they were very successful for both cod and conger eels. It might be worth noting that miniature versions of this spoon, about the size of a teaspoon bowl, will also enhance most bottom catches of ground fish like cod, whiting, spurs and even bass. In coloured water I am still not sure if the fish home in on the bait because of its visual attraction, or because of the vibrations of the spoon kicking in the tidal current—but for whatever reason they do and that they work should be enough for the angler!

Spoons and Spinners

At the smaller end of artificial lures are the metal spoons. Inexpensive when compared to heavy pirks, a spoon can be anything in weight up to two ounces. Strangely enough you have to send off to America to get any good flashing spoons of that weight, but if you want one up to one ounce in weight you should be able to get that at your local tackle shop.

One of the best makes to go for are the Ryobi Odin range of lures. They come in a wide variety of weights, finishes and highly effective

Sea Fishing Baits

colours and have a hard enamel finish. They will all catch mackerel, cod and pollock at some time or other, but as always there are some colours that are better for particular fish. The two colours I have had most success with are copper and silver—the copper Odin being best for pollock and the silver for mackerel and coalfish. They are all of limited use when boat fishing and are really for use when casting from the beach using light tackle.

Always allow a few seconds of sinking time before you start the retrieve, and try different speeds. Sometimes the fish want it fast, with a violent action, other times they take best with a slow seductive, injured fish look.

Shakespeare also offer a range of spinners and spoons. The better revolving blade spinners are the Jet or the Dorado, and the best of the spoons is the multi-coloured Blinker spoons, with silver or gold colours. They are sold as a freshwater pike spoon, but I assure you they work well enough for mackerel.

Then too you can't write about spoons and spinners without making mention of the famed Abu Toby's. It has been about for over thirty years and I hesitate to think how many fish it may have taken. The original Toby had a fluttering action and I have taken everything from perch to bonito on them, coming as they do in a wide variety of colours. Then there is the Toby tiger range, available in five sizes from 7 gm up to 28 gm. The original Toby comes in weights from 4 gms up to 28 gms. The Toby Salmo is catalogued as a salmon lure, but being heavier in weight, at 30 gm, it casts like a bullet, and will fish down deeper where the pollock and coalfish hide. This is the only size I would advise using from a boat, and then would limit its application to surface feeding bass that are pre-occupied with whitebait. A better lure for catching mackerel is the Toby Slim. This long lure casts quite well and comes in three sizes: 15, 20 and 28 gm. The heavier model is better, and must surely resemble a flashing sandeel as it is retrieved through the water. There is a lure called the Toby Fat, but it is nowhere near as successful as the others in this range.

The main difference between spinners and spoons is that the spinner will be much slower when fished, since it uses the water's

Artificials

friction to rotate the blade and give the lure some flash. This is fine, but the slower speed is uniform in direction and action and therefore gives those predators just that extra second or two to look at it—enough perhaps to make then realise it's just a piece of steel! At least with the spoon, the action allows a faster retrieve so that you can cut down the length of time a fish has to make that vital decision . . . of whether or not to take it.

As well as spoons, many of the modern pike angler's plugs can be used in the sea, though I hesitate to say to good effect because from my own experience spoons work far better. But should you decide to do some trolling inshore from a moving boat, the Rapala Magnum range are superb and have a violent, vibrating tail wiggle. They are also robust enough to stand up to the jaws of a big fish. When choosing a plug, try to go for the long slim ones rather than the short dumpy models. The slimmer ones resemble sandeels a little more, although they will not cast as far as a heavy 30-gm spoon.

Artificial lures definitely have a place in the modern angler's armoury, but I would think they are of greater use to the shore angler than his counterpart in the boat.

Bait Additives

I have mentioned before that I have a great liking for pilchard oil extract as a bait additive. Pilchard oil comes in concentrated or diluted form and can be purchased in bottles from your local tackle shop. However, as always the smaller the bottle you purchase the less value for money it will be. A pure fish oil extract is not cheap to make, so I would suggest several of you club together and buy a gallon (five-litre) bottle of pilchard oil from Brent's of Hailsham, Sussex. You can then keep this as your stock solution and bottle it down yourself into more manageable sizes perhaps into plastic washing up bottles—that can then be carried in your tackle box.

For the boat angler you can use it straight as it is, but a small tip here for shore anglers might put an extra fish or three on the beach. As everbody knows, oil floats, and pilchard oil is no exception. Although much of it stays on the bait and is not washed off as the bait hits the water, there will nevertheless be a surface slick where it entered the water. If you want more oil to stay down near the bottom where it will do the most good, you can made up a mix of pilchard oil and liquid emulsifier. Emulsifier is obtained from a tackle shop and is usually used by the carp angler in his bait mixes. The emulsifying agent will break down the oil and keep it nearer the bottom and therefore nearer the fish.

I personally use pilchard oil on both fish baits, and worms, especially lugworm. As I was finishing this book I went out off a Hampshire beach during a December neap tide (not the best for shore work, but it had to do) and I even took cod on ragworm which had been soused in pilchard oil—and fishing with two rods using identical bait and rigs, the one with oil consistently gave me more bites than the plain ragworm. Although I wasn't surprised by this and have complete faith in the oil, this was the first time I had conducted my own specific trial with a bait not usually associated with cod in the winter, and using a pair of rods, one with an oiled unit and one without. I suppose I could have been casting farther with one set of gear than the other, but I tried to gauge distances and cast them the same.

Now on to commercial products. Anglers have always longed for that magic elixir that will make their catches the envy of their friends,

Bait Additives

The cat-like eyes on this big bull huss are deceiving, for it locates its prey mostly by smell. An ideal species to respond to many of the new bait additives currently on the market.

Sea Fishing Baits

Why not try some of the freshwater angler's bait additives and flavourings. Not every additive need be fish based, although these would be the most obvious to start with.

and we have been seeing more and more of the 'instant fish or your money back' type of oils, juices and other things. You have 'Dr. Juice' time-release capsules, Berkley Strike which definitely has some fish oil in it, but looks like blue antifreeze! You have Chum N' Rub, which supposedly catches fish on a bare hook, and glows in the dark as an additional extra. There have even been synthetic lugworm and amino acid concentrates. Now I'm not saying they don't work, but none of them beat having a good fresh bait on the hook. What they are is an additive. Namely an additional smell factor or factors that might just enhance the natural smells your bait is already giving off. Of course not many anglers have stopped to think that it may also mask that natural scent, and thereby make it a less attractive bait.

I have tried almost every bait scent and additive that has ever come on the market. There is no wonder scent, only anglers who dream

Bait Additives

that there might be. You can't go out and buy a 50p bottle of twenty years' experience, because that's what makes a world-class sport-fisherman, not a magic bottle of jungle juice. There is only one scent that in my experience has proven to catch fish well and that's pilchard oil.

Doubtless much scientific work goes into manufacturing the new scents, but I promise you they will never catch fish that aren't there to be caught in the first place. Find your fish and you are three quarters of the way to a successful session. By all means buy a few bottles of the additives, but remember they are only trying to shortcut experience and skill. The skill with which you approach the collection, storage and use of your baits will give you far more satisfaction and probably more success than buying it in the tackle shop. And if you don't believe me, give it a try!

	Sandeel	Lance	Squid	Mackerel	Ragworm	Lugworm	Limpets	Crabs	Herring	Sprat	Razorfish	Artificial
Bass	X	X	X	X	X	X	X	X			X	X
Bream			X	X	X	X	X	X	X	X		
Cod	X	X	X	X	X	X	X	X	X	X	X	X
Conger			X	X					X	X		
Coalfish	X	X	X	X				X	X	X		X
Pollock	X	X	X	X				X	X	X		X
Flounder	X				X	X	X	X			X	
Plaice	X			X	X	X	X	X			X	
Dab					X	X	X		X		X	
Turbot	X		X	X					X	X		X
Megrim			X	X	X	X		X	X	X		
Ling			X	X				X	X	X		X
Haddock			X	X			X	X	X	X		
Mackerel	X				X	X						X
Rays		X	X	X	X	X		X	X	X	X	
Skate			X	X				X	X	X		
Tope		X	X	X			X	X	X			
Monkfish			X	X				X	X			
Dogfish	X	X	X	X	X	X		X	X	X	X	
Bull Huss			X	X				X	X	X		
Shark			X	X					X	X		

Table for popularity of each bait to different species